AMERICA
The Great

From now on,
Америка моя
(America is mine.)

Gerald Sprayregen
Editor and Designer

Printed in the United States of America by LSC Communications
First Printing, 2017

ISBN: 978-0-9852157-6-7

www.americathegreatthebook.com

Front cover illustration by Riber Hansson. Courtesy of Cagle Cartoons.
Back cover illustration by Ed Wexler. Courtesy of Cagle Cartoons.
Title page illustration by Michel Kichka.

Cover design by Suzanne Khalil and Deb Tremper

Acknowledgements

Numerous individuals who have made incredible contributions to this book have asked me to not mention their names because they fear some form of physical retaliation to themselves or their families by militant followers of our president, whose minds have been infiltrated by his inflammatory rhetoric. To these caring and talented friends, I send my love and appreciation for their dedication to this project. Their wisdom and hard work helped make *AMERICA THE GREAT* what it is.

A large number of individuals worked collectively as well as individually to bring this project to fruition. My warm and heartfelt thank you is extended to the individuals listed below alphabetically. Each has gone out of his/her way to help a first-time editor tell a story that many find unbelievable, even though it doesn't answer (indeed, makes more inexplicable the answer) to a simple question millions of people are asking each other, "How the hell did this happen?"

- Brian Fair at Cagle
- Richard Fronapfel
- Mitchell Kaplan
- Suzanne Khalil
- Alex Kriegsman
- Amy Lago
- Noelle-Claire LeCann
- Rick Marschall
- Hank Raattama
- Eric Rishell
- Seymour Sprayregen
- Marianne Sugawara
- Sara Thaves
- David Turner

I wish to give a very special thank you to Debra Tremper who, as my graphic designer, had the nearly impossible job of putting up with my never-ending requests, such as moving an item $1/16$ of an inch, and who always maintained her cool, even while I was bombarding her with twenty emails a day. Thank you dear Deb, you are fantastic.

And to the 52 artist heroes of *AMERICA THE GREAT*, my staff and I have found you each to have been a pleasure to work with. Your talent, your craft, your humor, your insight, your artistic abilities and your constant pleasant and optimistic viewpoints have made editing this group of approximately 200 important works of art an uplifting joy for me, while working 19–20 hour days, seven days a week since the beginning of this exciting project. The concepts, the beauty and the incredible humor of this art will go down in history as a definitive depiction of these times. The artists listed below have poured out their hearts and souls, and braved threats on their lives as well as having received applause from the majority of their readers. I send my sincere thank you to each of you for your honesty and incredible talent.

- Brian Adcock
- Jan-Erik Ander
- Nick Anderson
- Pat Bagley
- Nate Beeler
- Darrin Bell
- Clay Bennett
- Steve Benson
- Barry Blitt
- Steve Breen
- Steve Brodner
- Mark Bryan
- Pat Byrnes
- Daryl Cagle
- John Darkow
- Matt Davies
- Michael de Adder
- John Deering
- Liza Donnelly
- Bob Englehart
- Mark Fiore
- Dave Granlund
- Rainer Hachfeld
- Phil Hands
- Walt Handelsman
- Riber Hansson
- David Horsey
- Marian Kamensky
- Mike Keefe
- Michel Kichka
- Luo Jie
- Taylor Jones
- Mike Luckovich
- Olle Magnusson
- Andy Marlette
- RJ Matson
- Rick McKee
- Jim Morin
- Jack Ohman
- Joel Pett
- Andrew Rae
- Michael Ramirez
- David Rowe
- Steve Sack
- Gerald Scarfe
- Kevin Siers
- Tom Stiglich
- Ann Telnaes
- Ed Wexler
- Signe Wilkinson
- Matt Wuerker
- Adam Zyglis

Gerald Sprayregen

Dedication

I dedicate this book to every immigrant who has been mistreated by our current government, every big or small business person who has been forced into court by rich and powerful bullies, every woman who has been touched or insulted by a tyrant, every student who was swindled by a person or agency claiming to teach and help the young reach their goals, and every decent American who cries out for America to once again have our elected president have the moral fiber that our forefathers dreamed of when they penned our constitution in 1787!

I also dedicate this book to my twin brother, Seymour, who has been a tower of strength and support from conception to completion of this project. Seymour has been a diligent and an imaginative editor, and has worked on all written material in the book. Preceding this collaboration, Seymour has spent too much of his time caring and worrying about his older (by 10 minutes), mischievous brother. Besides my wonderful, beautiful mother and loving father, Seymour is the only person in my life who never gave up on me, regardless of my blunders and misdeeds.

Contents

Preface
by Rick Marschall

Editorial cartooning, specifically political cartooning, thrives at times of urgent public debates and vivid personalities.

Cartoons also, in turn, have influenced history. Napoleon said that history is written by the victors—and it is just as true that our views of history often have been shaped by artists, including cartoonists.

Much of what we think and know (or think we know) of kings, presidents, generals, candidates, and leaders of movements has been codified by cartoonists. Oftentimes, major figures in history have been portrayed to their detriment—sometimes unfairly and sometimes falsely. No matter, our opinions of, say, Andrew Jackson or Williams Jennings Bryan largely are what the cartoonists said through their art.

Time will tell if we are entering a new Golden Age of political cartooning, but many signs are at hand. The Trump presidency, indeed the Trump phenomenon, provides an unprecedented opportunity for political cartoonists to spread their ink-stained wings as seldom seen before.

At a conference held by the Association of American Editorial Cartoonists in the mid-1970s, Meg Greenfield of the *Washington Post* addressed the assembled cartoonists and thanked them for providing "laughs" and "morning chuckles." The assembled cartoonists mostly were outraged that after investing in careers as pictorial commentators, they were being dismissed as court jesters.

It was outrageous that someone from the staff of the newspaper home of Herblock could so totally misunderstand the unique gift—the art—of the political cartoon. Maybe cartoonists make their points through laughs, but that one creative tool among many others is not the only special attribute of cartoons—there is the ideal of truth itself.

In the Age of Trump, the responsibility of the reader is as profound as the responsibility of the cartoonist. We now turn to the history of the caricatured leader.

The history of the presidential cartoon had its origins in lies, propaganda, and extreme partisanship. A strange beginning? It is the hallmark of caricatures and cartoons to attack, not endorse.

Yet the sensitivity and frustrations of public enemies were summed up by the leader of New York City's Democratic "machine," Tammany Hall, around 1871, "I don't care what the papers write about me; my people can't read. But, damn it, they can see pictures!"

The first American political cartoon, "Join or Die," by Benjamin Franklin, of all people, was a polemical argument, an appeal to reason, cleverly composed. But on its heels was Paul Revere's engraving of the Boston Massacre, an incendiary a piece of nonsense as was ever produced by any pen or any word. It was presented by Revere as a documentary depiction of a massacre. It was closer to a confused mob scene, yet it inflamed Colonists when the Colonies needed inflammation.

The political cartoon, not for the last time in our history, was the spark that inflamed the tinder of public opinion. Sometimes *a* spark, occasionally *the* spark.

Largely forgotten by history is the fact that the Father of Our Country frequently was attacked as harboring ambitions to be a monarch; that he surrounded himself with what were deemed odious sycophants like Hamilton and

Benjamin Franklin's famous and iconic "Join or Die" cartoon ran many times in many formats (for instance, as components of newspapers' logos and as handbills) between the French and Indian War and the Articles of Confederation.

Paul Revere engraved this pictorial propaganda, otherwise known as an effective political cartoon, exaggerating the conflict between British troops and patriots. It became known as the Boston Massacre, inflaming passions for a war with England.

Thomas Jefferson, a drunken madman in league with the Devil, is depicted in this cartoon as threatening the federal government as established by Washington and Adams. Anonymous cartoonist.

Adams. Criticisms of Hamilton were not above referring to his bastard birth, supposed libertine habits, and rumored mixed-race blood.

Criticisms also were leveled in print and crude drawings against Thomas Jefferson, another figure whose spotted reputation had been sanitized through the decades. Jeffersonians variously were portrayed as uneducated, anti-social, French anarchists, atheistic, and libertine. Even when these characteristics were accurate, political cartoonists answered in kind. The press of Jefferson's party took to making false and defamatory statements…but received as often as they gave.

In our early history, other icons developed in the form of cartoonists' Ograbme—a snapping turtle whose image and name, "Embargo" in reverse, suggested the self-defeating aspect of Jefferson's policy of avoiding trade with England and France during one of their wars. Later, the outline of a redrawn electoral map that favored Massachusetts governor Elbridge Gerry—the districts resembling the shape of a salamander—inspired a cartoonist to create an iconic lizard-like creature, the Gerrymander. The name has stuck.

Uncle Sam, originally represented by the female Columbia, and then as Brother Jonathan, is perhaps the political cartoonists' greatest icon, followed by the Democrat donkey and the Republican elephant. (Eventually the austere Mr. Prohibition, or the dry camel, dominated the 1920s, as Herblock's Mr. A-Bomb monopolized the 1950s. Vaughn Shoemaker created the iconic John Q. Public—you and me—a character adopted by other cartoonists.)

Comparisons have been drawn between Andrew Jackson and Donald Trump, not the least by Trump himself, who arranged the Oval Office so Old Hickory would gaze over his shoulder. Jackson was a populist and iconoclast who defied parties and the establishment. He could be vulgar, had "complicated" personal histories with finances and women, and shifting alliances.

The snapping turtle "Ograbme" (embargo spelled backwards) was an early cartoon mascot of many through the years. The issue was Jefferson's prescription of avoiding all trade so not to inflame Britain or France, who were at war. It was characteristic of Jefferson's weak foreign-policy views—it failed and was withdrawn. This cartoon by Alexander Anderson was persuasive in opposition arguments.

Cartoonist Elkanah Tisdale was impressed that a crazy bit of re-districting in Massachusetts's Essex County, favorable to Elbridge Gerry's political hopes, resembled a salamander. Hence was born a cartoon mascot and a permanent term in American politics: The Gerrymander (1812).

Cartoonist David Claypool Johnston depicted Senator Henry Clay as sewing President Andrew Jackson's mouth shut ("lockjaw") for the Senate's censure of Jackson's move to disestablish the Second National Bank of the United States.

The Rats leaving a Falling House.

This is another anti-Jackson cartoon (see above). Today the Peggy Eaton affair would be a sex scandal. It was the same thing in the 1830s. Peggy's questionable past and even more scandalous present resulted in the resignations of all Cabinet members but one. This cartoon, by Edward Williams Clay, depicts that situation, but Jackson was re-elected.

Anti-Jackson cartoons often depicted him as a murderous drunk or a libertine consorting with ruffians. Jackson opened himself to such characterizations because, among other items on his resume, he had killed men in battle and in duels; was likely guilty of bigamy; had the White House bar open to the public who trashed its ballrooms on Inauguration night; and so forth. A pretty Washington girl with a questionable past married a cabinet secretary and was rumored to "entertain" at cabinet sessions. All the cabinet but one member resigned, and cartoonists had a field day with the national scandal.

Jackson defied the Establishment by opposing the Second National Bank and the Eastern "money interests." In a protracted political and economic battle (a battle Jackson ultimately won), a Depression was precipitated. Cartoonists on both sides of the issues unleashed effective broadsides.

After the controversies and scandals of Andrew Jackson's two terms, slavery asserted itself…and breathed life into cartoons.

III.

In the 1840s, images, portraits, icons, and caricatures showed up on banners, torchlight-parade paraphernalia, lapel pins, one-sheet penny cartoons, and (usually crude) humor-magazine cartoons.

The Civil War represents a perfect storm in the lifeline of political cartooning. Advances in woodcutting enabled numerous, and rapidly produced, cartoons to fill page after page of *Harper's Weekly*, *Leslie's Weekly*, and other papers. Artists drew their cartoons, illustrations, and war-sketches on boxwood, to be engraved.

The prominent figures of the era dominated the political cartoons. Such figures included Abraham Lincoln and his cabinet, especially Secretary of State William Seward. On the Confederate side, President Jefferson Davis frequently was caricatured, as were the diminutive Vice President Stephens and the corpulent Treasury Secretary Judah Benjamin. Just as frequently, symbols populated political cartoons: the American Eagle, Uncle Sam, loathsome slave masters, and degraded slaves.

This cartoon is brilliant in its simplicity and venom. *Vanity Fair*, an anti-Lincoln weekly, made hay of the story that President-elect Lincoln, on the train to take office in Washington, feared angry pro-Secession mobs in Baltimore…and disguised himself in a cloak and Scottish cap. Whether true or not, "The New President of the United States" was a cartoon widely circulated ridiculing Lincoln in 1861.

Lincoln proved to be a special case in the annals of presidential cartoons. His popularity, even in the North, varied and sometimes was grudging. *Harper's Weekly*, for instance, which was virtually the voice of the war effort and the new Republican Party, often depicted Lincoln as a rangy, scruffy, uncouth backwoodsman—which, to an extent, he was.

And now we come to the first great American political cartoonist, Thomas Nast. A young artist from Bavaria, Nast originally drew random news and allegorical drawings that quickly morphed into Allegories Writ Large, cartoons of strong advocacy. President Lincoln eventually called Nast "The Union's best recruiting sergeant" for his effective, patriotic cartoons.

Arguably the most famous political cartoons in American history were Nast's post-war series of attacks against "Boss" Tweed and his cronies in the corrupt New York City Democrat organization known as the Tweed "Ring" in 1871. Thomas Nast took the political club's mascot, the face of a tiger, and gave it life as a rapacious beast attacking Justice and plundering the city's treasury. Week after week in *Harper's Weekly,* Nast drew savage cartoons that exposed the Ring and attracted widespread attention.

In the elections of November 1871, much of the Ring, state and city Democrat officials, were voted out of office. Eventually Tweed and others were sent to jail, largely due to Thomas Nast.

Scarcely more than a decade later, a presidential election was decided to a major extent by political cartoons. The Republican presidential candidate,

Another clever cartoon requiring few labels or captions was this *Harper's Weekly* cartoon from the 1864 re-election campaign. "This reminds me of a little joke" plays out as a double pun and simultaneously references Lincoln's propensity to tell jokes. The general is shown symbolically diminutive and Lincoln's failed General George B. McClellan was the Democratic candidate. He was to lose by a wide margin, but he was as short as Lincoln was tall.

At the height of his powers in 1871, Thomas Nast of *Harper's Weekly* caricatured and exposed the Democrat Boss of New York City and his corrupt "Tammany Ring." So skillful was Nast that by subtly arranging a dollar sign and replacing a bag of money for Tweed's head, he was instantly recognizable.

The weekly cartoons of Nast against the corrupt Tweed Ring eventually led to their political rout in the New York City municipal elections of 1871. The public had been educated (and revolted) by the corruption. Just before election day (when, in fact, almost all the Democrat office-holders and cronies of Tweed were defeated), this cartoon ran full-page in *Harper's Weekly* with the caption: "A group of vultures waiting for the storm to blow over—'Let Us Prey.'"

This cartoon by Bernhard Gillam was one of the most prominent cartoons in the "Tattooed Man" series from the 1884 presidential election. The GOP candidate was James G. Blaine.

In the same dirty campaign, Republicans answered with nasty cartoons of their own. Frank Beard, in *Judge*, found a cartoonist's way of addressing the rumors that Democrat Grover Cleveland had fathered an illegitimate child, "Another Voice for Cleveland." The rumors were true; he confessed forthrightly, and the Victorian-era public forgave him, electing him president three times (in 1888 he lost the electoral college).

James G. Blaine, was a first-class scoundrel with a trail of documented corruption during his career in politics (which included his role as Speaker of the House). Yet his personal magnetism and political debts secured the GOP nomination in 1884.

After a generation of political corruption in America, culminating in the assassination of President James A. Garfield by an office-seeker of a rival political faction, reform was in the air. The Democrats nominated the "ugly honest" freshman governor of New York, Grover Cleveland. A realignment of political classes occurred, with many prominent Republicans (for instance, Nast and the *Weekly*) switching support to Cleveland, who later credited the political cartoons in *Puck* with having elected him.

Since the late 1850s, Currier and Ives, "Printmakers to the American people," had issued penny prints of political cartoons—on order, and therefore attacking and championing all candidates. When Joseph Keppler founded *Puck* magazine in 1876, he took Currier and Ives' novelties to a new height: he managed a front page, center spread, and back page of cartoons, lithographed in color. *Puck* became the first successful political cartoon weekly in America. The magazine also featured literary humor and social satire. It successfully was copied by *Judge* (which was Republican, whereas *Puck* leaned Democrat) and the black-and-white cartoon weekly *Life*.

A presidential election of unprecedented vituperation occurred in 1896. Cartoonists in 1884 correctly had identified the major issue then of systemic corruption and personal scandals; but in 1896, the nation as a whole, and even the competing parties and candidates, smelled social revolution in the air.

William Jennings Bryan, at 36 years of age, had barely passed the Constitutional age requirement (35) to be president when he swept the Democrat convention with a speech opposed to the gold standard. America was in a deep economic depression, and for a generation, farmers and Western settlers had

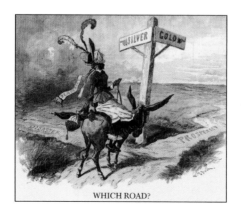

Democracy was pictured at the crossroads in this 1895 cartoon by C. G. Bush in the *New York Herald*. There was a crushing Depression, labor and social unrest, a Populist party vying for power, and demands for inflated currency.

advocated for silver coinage and against inflation and Wall Street. Bryan, who also favored an income tax and inheritance taxes, was depicted as an unbalanced revolutionary at best, a murderous anarchist at worst. Democrat cartoonists of *Puck*, *New York World*, and *New York Herald* became Republicans for a reason. Even the incumbent president Cleveland refused to support Bryan.

The Republican recipient of this turmoil was William McKinley. Supported by virtually every political cartoonist in the country (except for those of publishing tycoon William Randolph Hearst), McKinley was elected. Prosperity returned, and so eventually did partisanship among the political cartooning profession.

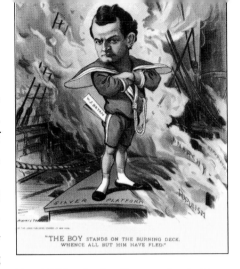

"THE BOY STANDS ON THE BURNING DECK. WHENCE ALL BUT HIM HAVE FLED."

Though William Jennings Bryan was barely old enough to run for president, a Populist speech at the Democrat convention cased a stampede in his favor. Hardly a cartoon showed him as mature, or without stormy skies in the background, or without a pocketful of revolutionary ideas...most of which were accepted and commonplace within a generation. The cartoon above was illustrated by Grant Hamilton and appeared in *Judge* (1896).

IV.

The Modern Era in America—the "American Century," the modern presidency, and Uncle Sam as a world player—coincided with the turn of the last century and the presidency of Theodore Roosevelt.

Political cartoonists' influence increased a million-fold in the daily press. Frederick Opper, Homer Davenport, Charles Green Bush, and John T. McCutcheon became household names whose opinions were as influential as any politician's or columnist's.

President Theodore Roosevelt arguably was the most caricatured president in history. The effervescent Theodore Roosevelt at age 42 was the youngest man to serve as president (still the case), and was, as the author and exemplar of "The Strenuous Life," a constant subject for cartoonists. As a former legislator, historian, author, cowboy, Washington reformer, police commissioner, hero soldier (as "Rough Rider"), governor of New York and Vice President, he was a multi-faceted subject. With his exuberance, eyeglasses, mustache, and snapping teeth, he was also a perfect candidate for caricature.

"He's Good Enough For Me!"

From the N. Y. Evening Mail

Even opposition cartoonists and writers seldom failed to capture the exuberance and boisterous enthusiasm of Theodore Roosevelt. In 1910, cartoonist W. A. Carson of the Utica (NY) *Saturday Globe* depicted TR's unexpected capture of the New York State GOP after his return from a post-presidency African safari and grand tour of Europe.

This cartoon was one of the most famous and effective political cartoons in American history. In the 1904 presidential campaign, this was used as a document of Homer Davenport's friendship with and support of Theodore Roosevelt after having attacked Roosevelt for years.

Theodore Roosevelt identifies a "Weak Fish," President Wilson, to the Army and Navy, referring to Wilson's defense reductions while Europe was at war. William H. Walker in *Life*, 1916.

Life magazine depicted President Wilson as a prissy pacifist who endured diplomatic and military insults during America's "neutrality" before the U.S. intervened in the Great War. William H. Walker, 1915.

President Roosevelt stimulated, indeed invited, many controversies, which in their turn provided additional fodder for political cartoonists. Trust busting, conservation, managing the Panama Canal, winning the Nobel Peace Prize, settling labor strikes, establishing regulatory reforms, advocating a strong navy… Theodore Roosevelt provided political cartoonists with a host of subjects to depict and analyze.

The 'teens can be remembered as the period of Woodrow Wilson (whose brand of Progressivism was different than Roosevelt's and ultimately the brand we know today), and for World War I. Wilson's treatment by political cartoonists was unremarkable, settling into predictable partisan camps.

During World War I, the federal government, as part of its attempted mobilization of everything in sight, created the Division of Pictorial Publicity. Under the leadership of cartoonist Charles Dana Gibson, political cartoonists, comic-strip artists, and illustrators created posters and drew pro-war cartoons for newspapers, magazines, and billboards.

V.

The nature of political cartooning changed when the nature of the American presidency changed with Franklin D. Roosevelt. Issues of the Depression, dislocation, collectivism, isolationism, and the Second World War, were, as much as FDR himself, responsible for a new focus in political cartooning.

But FDR also consciously presented himself as a "personality," a magnet to political cartoonists, who have tended ever since to focus on the "man," not so much the vague "nation" or "administration." Today, cartoonists will still

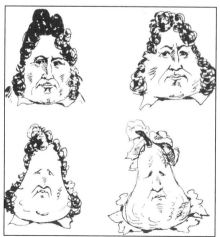

French King Louis-Philippe in 1830 banned caricatures of his royal self and began to close publications and arrest cartoonists. Cartoonist Charles Philipon, caricaturist and founder of several papers, was threatened after lampooning the king. At his trial, he drew the face of the king transforming himself into a pear, which is how he drew him thereafter. He asked the jury: "Is it my fault if His Majesty looks like a pear?" He was acquitted of defamation.

A famous anti-war, anti-FDR cartoon because of its theme and timing, "The Colors" ran in 1939 as Franklin Roosevelt was ramping up efforts to intervene in the European conflict. More than 85% of the American public was anti-intervention. The *Chicago Tribune* ran this color cartoon by John McCutcheon (multiple Pulitzer Prize-Winner) full page, multiple times.

Cartoonist Jean Veber got the magazine *L'Assiette au Beurre* temporarily banned for drawing British King Edward VII's face on the posterior of Britannia in 1901. A factor in the state's case was that the king was about to pay a state visit to France.

Art Young was the most prominent and longest-serving radical cartoonist in America. Although he drew humor cartoons for *The Saturday Evening Post* and *The New Yorker*, most of his work was for magazines like *The Masses* (several of whose staffers were arrested along with him on charges of sedition during World War I) and obscure protest publications. This cartoon, which he called his favorite, was for *Puck*, circa 1907, about New York's Episcopal Church as slumlord.

call upon Uncle Sam and the donkey and elephant (as the parties themselves do in their logos)—yet there has been greater use of individual presidential caricatures.

Presidents have encouraged this association, of course. Theodore Roosevelt was the first president bold enough to brand his policies (the Square Deal), and Wilson, who often picked Theodore Roosevelt's pocket in various initiatives, called his program the "New Freedom." Then the evolving nature of the presidency, and therefore the reactions of political cartoonists, can be tracked through the brand names: the "New Deal," the "Fair Deal," the "New Frontier," the "Great Society," and so forth.

The New Deal and World War II naturally excited passions and inspired cartoons for and against Franklin Roosevelt and his policies. His risk, laying himself open to the barbs as well as the attention and commendations of political cartoonists, was successful to the extent that he became the target of political cartoons. He had many supporters in the press, but opposition political

"Army Medical Examiner: 'At last a perfect soldier!'"

The father of radical political cartooning in America might be Robert Minor. As a staff cartoonist for the *St. Louis Post-Dispatch* and the *New York World*, he drew attractive cartoons, resurrecting the use of grease crayons as European cartoonists were using. When Minor veered to radicalism around 1912, he helped found *The Masses* and soon gave up cartooning for the Communist Party—the party for which he then ran for several political offices.

Franklin Roosevelt enjoyed public support at the start of the New Deal, but many newspapers and cartoonists opposed him, especially as agencies and programs proliferated. Lute Pease in the *Newark News* criticized FDR's economic tinkering, circa 1935.

cartoonists often depicted him as a fool or a subversive, a megalomaniac or dictator. Conservative cartoonists drew strong personal attacks on FDR all through the Depression and War, until his death.

With Eisenhower, the bland uncle in the White House did not escape the ridicule of opponents among political cartoonists. His detractors, who in the post-war, Cold War era included names like Herblock and Bill Mauldin, depicted Ike as a vacuous fool.

During the Cold War, Herb Block ("Herblock") was the art form's major cartoonist, and many artists copied his style…and shared his targets—Ike, Senator Joseph McCarthy, and famously, Richard Nixon. After portraying Nixon as a brigand with a heavy five-o'clock shadow and crawling up from sewers (in a cartoon that Nixon publicly criticized as hurtful for his daughters to see), Herblock drew one of the great and iconic political cartoons—simply, a barber chair with the Washington skyline out the window and a sign which pledged a "clean shave" to all new presidents—that is, a new beginning.

John F. Kennedy was narrowly elected in 1960 but enjoyed an amazing honeymoon with the public and with political cartoonists. His vision, optimistic legislative agenda, and call for vigor ("vigah," reminiscent of Theodore Roosevelt's "Strenuous Life") were the fodder for many cartoonists.

By the end of Lyndon Johnson's presidency—a cauldron of controversial social legislation ("The Great Society") and the divisive Vietnam War—Johnson lost much of his support from a sympathetic press and corps of cartoonists. In a period riven by several assassinations, mass protests, urban riots, and political scandals, the profession of political cartooning became more vicious than ever.

By 1936, many of FDR's original supporters in the press and public—and backers like the radio priest Father Coughlin, and populist senator Huey Long—abandoned the New Deal. Powerful voices of the left and right opposed FDR, yet his 1936 re-election was by a landslide. Thomas Carlisle, circa 1936, *New York Herald Tribune*.

President Harry Truman's honeymoon with the American public was short-lived after the death of FDR. This 1946 cartoon by Shoemaker refers to missed economic projections by Truman, the former haberdasher. The cartoonist was famous for creating his "own" Uncle Sam—John Q. Public, an icon borrowed by many other cartoonists.

Franklin Delano Roosevelt's initial support among segments of the political landscape, from the left to the right, cooled as the number and enormity of New Deal programs became evident. Among the cartoonists who became skeptical was Vaughn Shoemaker. This cartoon (above) was drawn by Shoemaker during midterm elections, 1938.

Above is a cartoon by Herblock that offended Vice President Richard Nixon in 1954. It appeared in the *Washington Post*.

At this time, a new breed of political cartoonists was heralded by Pat Oliphant's arrival from Australia. America had never had a cartoonist who was funnier or more scathingly brutal in making prescient points—often simultaneously. He often couched his concepts as captioned gags; he seldom used labels but was comfortable to call upon Uncle Sam when appropriate. With Oliphant, Nixon was evil, Carter was a dunce, Reagan was an airhead, (George H.W.) Bush was effeminate, and (Bill) Clinton was a hillbilly manipulator…

Jeff MacNelly proved to be the ablest stylistic disciple of Oliphant—a brilliant advocate and artist who was as effective on the Right as Oliphant was on the Left. Herblock and Bill Mauldin continued in their trademark ways. (Mauldin had become a mainstay of political cartooning beginning with his days in the European Theater in World War II, with his Willie and Joe characters.)

Not only Oliphant but virtually every political cartoonist in the land (at least eventually) joined the chorus of Nixon detractors. Columnists, comedians, and other politicians, all roasted the disgraced Nixon…but his downfall, indeed his very personality, is defined by the brutal and brilliant caricatures of Herblock, Oliphant, David Levine, Paul Conrad, and Ralph Steadman.

A fitting "wrap" to the historical processes that have brought political cartooning to the Age of Trump is this reference to the "clean shave" that Herblock famously pledged to the incoming President Richard Nixon. This caricature of Herb Block by Bill Watterson (later the creator of *Calvin and Hobbes*) for Richard West's magazine *Target* shows the best practitioners of the art practicing what they do best—or should do best: pledging that every cartoon, every day, will be new and fresh…but never without the sharpened razor, next to the pen and brush.

President Jimmy Carter scarcely felt safe after narrowly beating back primary challenges from Senator Ted Kennedy. Cartoonist Pat Oliphant recalled Chappaquiddick and the fate of other back-seat drivers.

Cartoonist Jeff MacNelly recalled several great American presidents and words they will be remembered for.

VI.

Ronald Reagan precipitated a slow shift toward more conservatives entering the political cartooning field (traditionally dominated by liberals, now virtually balanced by conservatives), mirroring the trends in the country. His opponents among political cartoonists variously depicted him as a dunce or a maniacal warmonger, as the issues required.

The Bushes (George H.W., "Bush One" and George W., "Bush Two') might go down in history as bookends to the Clinton years. Father and son largely were dismissed by the majority of political cartoonists as lightweights. Oliphant's ever-present purse on Bush One's arm was an icon that spoke volumes; and, except for the immediate responses to 9-11, Bush Two was depicted as a clueless Republican version of Jimmy Carter who was in over his head. (Carter also suffered from slights, even by many Democrats and liberal cartoonists.)

Barack Obama's political body is still warm and the memories of his treatment by political cartoonists are fresh. There was much speculation about how he would be depicted by a profession whose lifeblood is stereotypes, cliches, signs, and symbols. But this was the 21st century, and as the first black president, he was generally immune from demeaning caricatures. A growing segment of conservative cartoonists did not pull punches, but his depictions were confined to big ears, long face, and trademark insouciance ("No Drama Obama"). His legacy is fresh and as controversial as ever, so beyond the scope of this essay, and sets a prelude to the cartoons collected here.

But the relevant question remains how—and how well, how effectively, and with what impact—contemporary political cartoonists ply their unique trade today. The Age of Trump has provided an unprecedented supply of material—a unique moment in American history.

The controversies and cartoons in the book that follows are examples of the alchemy, not only the art form, that is political cartooning. These artists are advocates. Also, at their core, they are observers. They observe for us and prompt us to observe more wisely. Their work—this book—is a chronicle of the times.

And what times they are!

Rick Marschall, a former political cartoonist (William Loeb's Connecticut Herald*) and political columnist, is the author of 74 books including cartoon histories and anthologies. He has been editor of Marvel Comics, a writer for Disney, editor at three newspaper syndicates, and has taught at Rutgers, the School of Visual Arts, the University of the Arts/PCA, and the Summer Institute For the Gifted at Bryn Mawr. He was consultant for 20 commemorative stamps of the U.S. Postal Service featuring cartoons; and has spoken abroad for the U.S. Information Service of the Department of State.*

AMERICA
The Great

Riber Hansson

Riber Hansson has been a newspaper artist for over three decades in the Swedish newspapers *Dagens Industri*, *Svenska Dagbladet*, and *Sydsvenskan*—the latter his main publisher even today. His works also appear occasionally in international media.

Many of his works have been shown in exhibitions, and selected drawings are collected in books. Hansson has had seventeen one-man exhibitions and has contributed to more than forty group exhibitions. He has received sixteen awards for his drawings. The most important are the World Press Cartoon's Grand Prix, the World Press Cartoon's second place in editorial cartoons, the World Press Cartoon's third place in caricature which he received twice, the first Press Cartoon Europe's Grand Prix, and the first Swedish EWK-award in 2000. Three books with his own editorial cartoons have been published, in addition to the five books published in cooperation with other authors. He has done book covers and illustrations for more than thirty books for children and adults. His work is available in North America through Cagle Cartoons Syndicate.

The artist prefers to relax by painting, drawing, reading, and writing.

Caglecartoons.com

Taylor Jones

Taylor Jones is one of America's premier pen and ink political illustrators and a master of watercolors. Currently, he draws caricatures, editorial cartoons, and illustrations for the *Hoover Digest* and Puerto Rico's largest newspaper, *El Nuevo Dia*. He is a former illustrator of the "Washington Whispers" page of *U.S. News & World Report*. He is a member of The Association of American Editorial Cartoonists, The National Cartoonist Society, and The Society of Illustrators.

Jones's work is nationally syndicated to over 1,000 newspapers and websites by Cagle Cartoons Newspaper Syndicate.

Jones is the author of *Add-Verse to Presidents* (Norton, 1982), a satirical look at the presidency from Washington to Reagan. He illustrated and designed a series of books on the lexicon of professional sports, including *How to Talk Baseball* (Galahad Books, 1996), and *How to Talk Golf* (Dembner Books, 1983).

Taylor Jones lives on Staten Island, New York.

THE DONALD J. TRUMP FOUNDATION

5

7

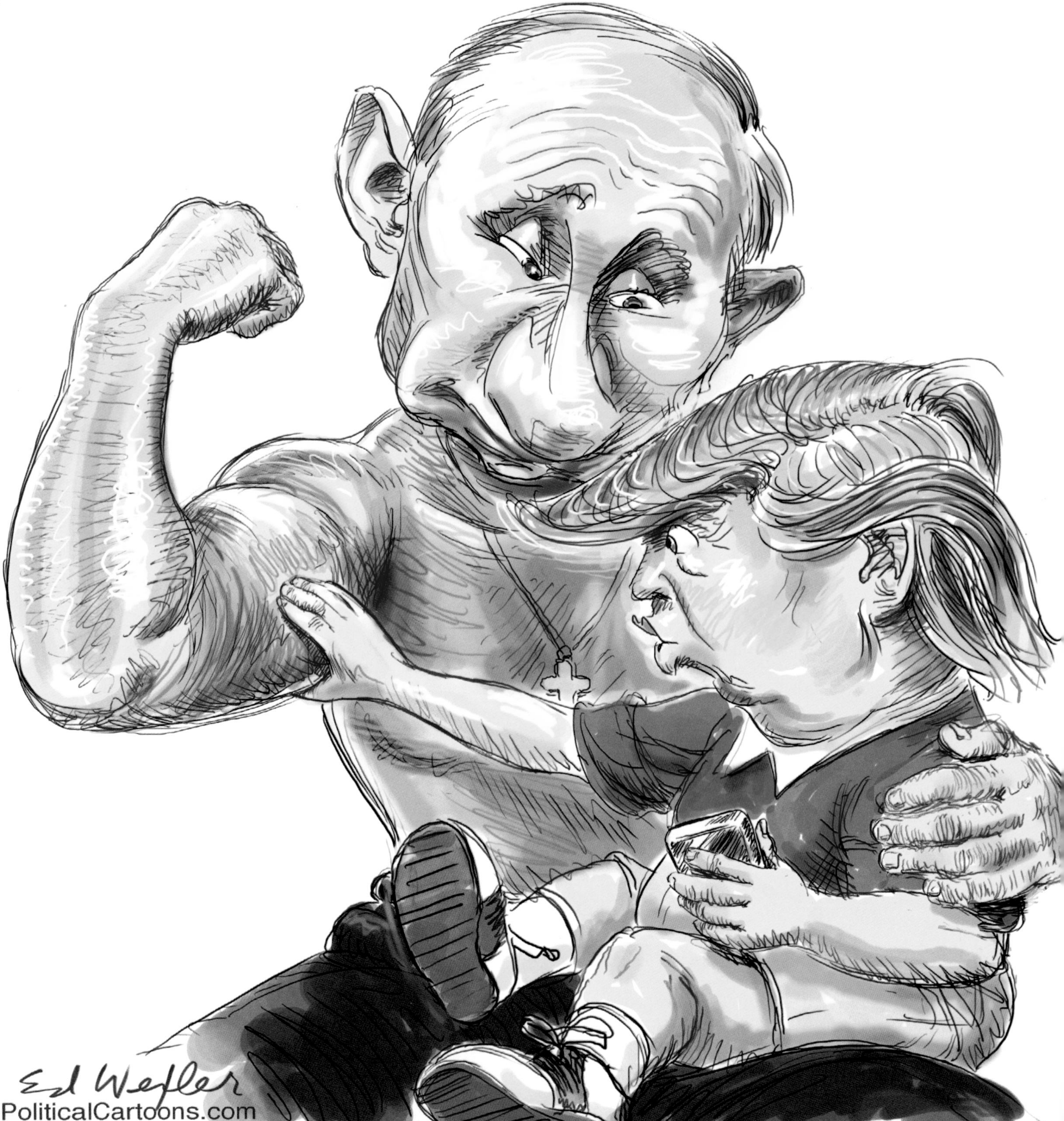
Ed Wexler
PoliticalCartoons.com

Ed Wexler

Ed Wexler is a first-class illustrator and animator who has mastered a variety of fields during his impressive career. He has been inspired by renowned contemporary illustrators such as David Levine and Ari Hirscfield.

Wexler worked at the Walt Disney Company from 1984 to 2004, and also had a long stint as an illustrator of *U.S. News & World Report*. During his time at Disney Studios, Wexler was known for his work on *DuckTales* (1987), *Winnie the Pooh: A Very Merry Pooh Year* (2002) and *In the Bleachers* (2002) just to name a few. Over the past several years, Wexler's commissioned work for the *Hollywood Reporter's* special Emmy and Academy Awards issues has earned him a reputation as being among the best caricature artists working in print today.

His editorial cartoons are nationally syndicated by Cagle Cartoons.

Wexler currently resides in southern California.

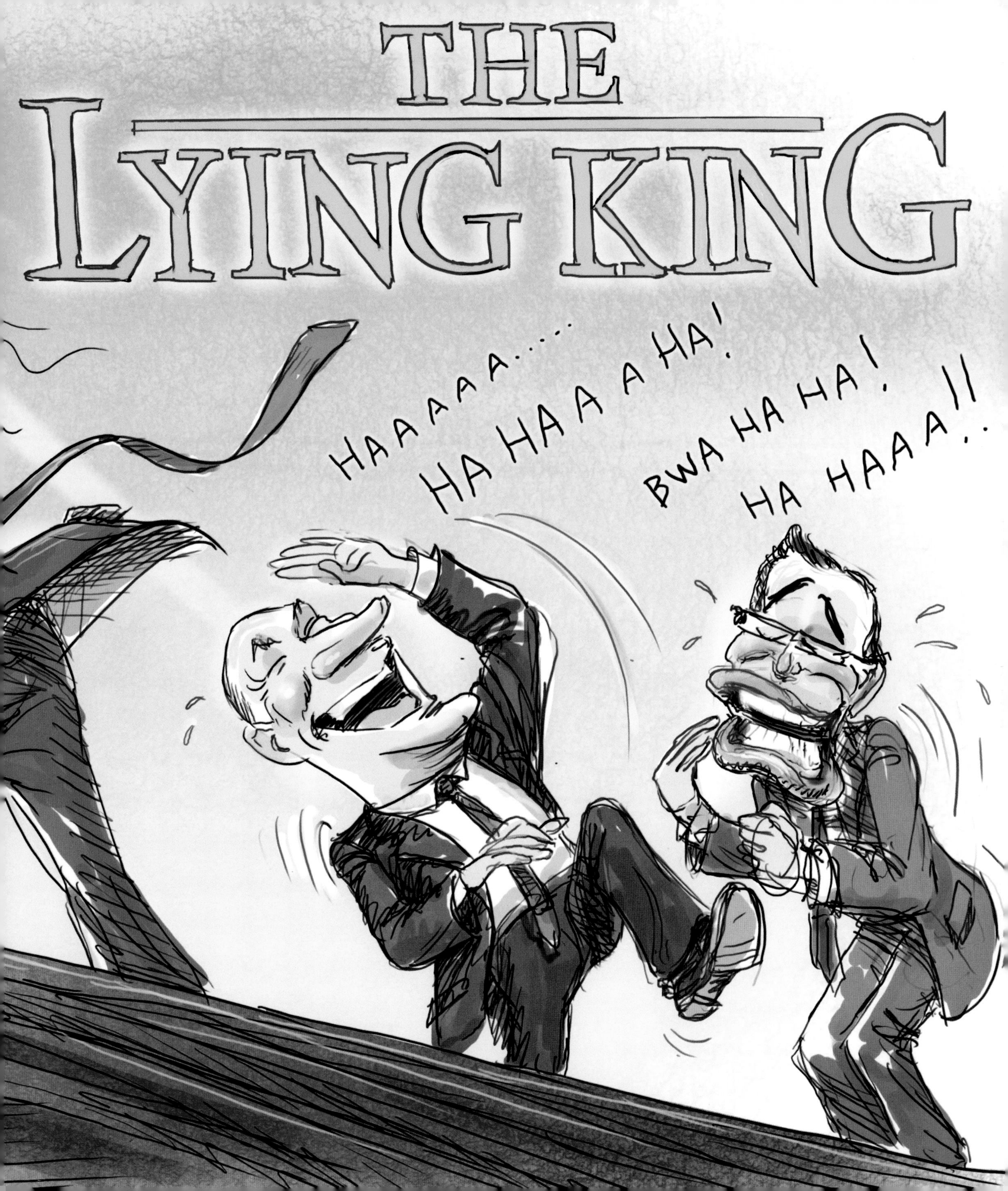
THE LYING KING
HAAAAA......
HA HAA A A HA!
BWA HA HA HA!
HA HAAA!!..

John Deering

John Deering is chief editorial cartoonist for the *Arkansas Democrat-Gazette*, Arkansas's largest newspaper. His cartoon comments entertain (and sometimes enrage) readers throughout Arkansas, Washington, D.C., and across the country.

Deering has been drawing since childhood. He put his fascination for science fiction and dinosaurs into comic books. After studying art with Truman Alston, Deering focused on commercial and fine art at the University of Arkansas at Little Rock. While there, he found his strength in interlocking art with comment. At the *Democrat-Gazette*, Deering advanced from layout artist to editorial cartoonist in 1981–82. His promotion to chief editorial cartoonist in 1988 made his cartoons the state's best-known.

Winner of the National Press Foundation's 1997 Berryman Award, Deering also gained top honors in the 1994 national John Fischetti Cartoon Competition and was the seven-time winner of the Arkansas Press Association's Best Editorial Cartoonist award. Deering's work is collected in two books: *Deering's State of Mind* (1990) and *We Knew Bill Clinton…Bill Clinton Was a Friend of Ours* with Vic Harville (1993). He is a fourteen-year member of the American Association of Editorial Cartoonists.

Deering also creates the comic panel *Too Much Coffee*. He and his wife, Kathy, have a daughter and two sons, and live in Little Rock. He still draws dinosaurs. Check out his comic strips, *Zack Hill* and *Strange Brew*.

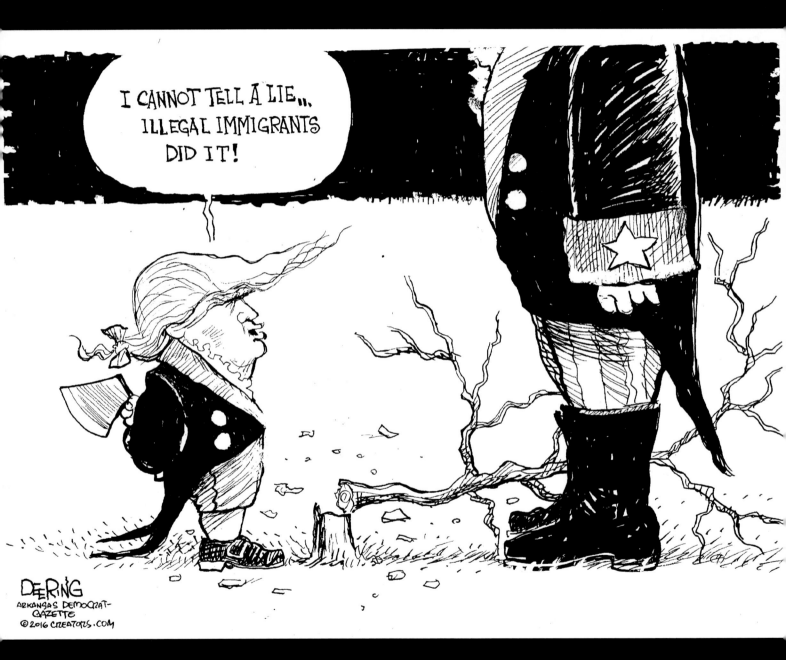

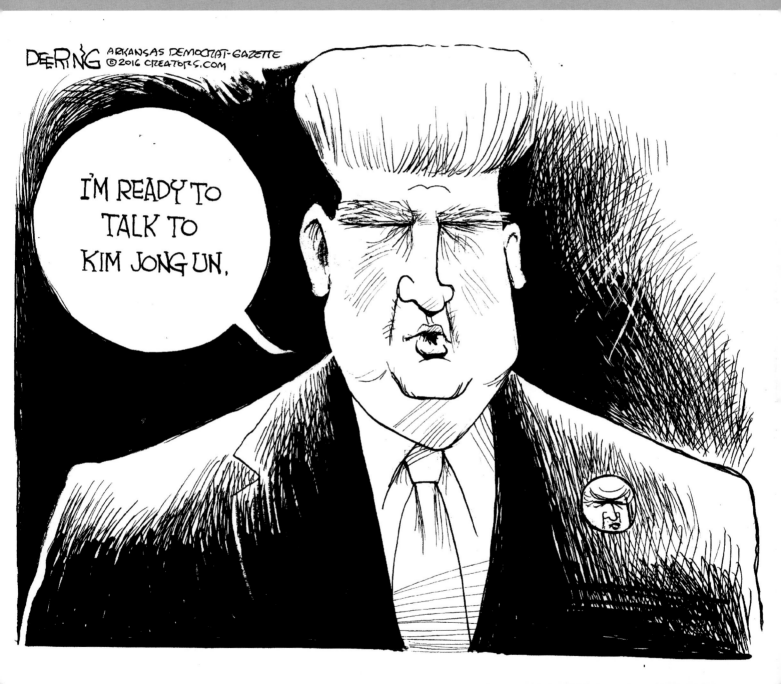

Mike Luckovich

Mike Luckovich, born January 1960, is an award-winning editorial cartoonist whose cartoons appear regularly in *Newsweek*, *Time*, the *Washington Post*, and over 150 other United States newspapers. Luckovich has worked with the *Greenville News* (1984–85), the *New Orleans Times-Picayune* (1985–1989), and has been with the *Atlanta Journal Constitution* since 1989.

Luckovich was a Pulitzer Prize award finalist in 1986 and has won the following prestigious awards: Overseas Press Club Winner (1990 & 1993), National Headliner Award Winner (1992), Robert F. Kennedy Award for cartoons which reflect positively on the disadvantaged (1994), The Pulitzer Prize (1995 & 2006), The Rueben Award for Outstanding Cartoonist of the Year (2006) Awarded by the National Cartoonist Society, The National Headliner Award (2006), The Thomas Nast Award (2006), and The Sigma Delta Chi Award (2006). Books include, *Lotsa Luckovich*, published by Simon and Schuster in 1996, and *Four More Wars*, published in 2006.

The online New Georgia Encyclopedia's entry on Luckovich, tells of an interaction with Bill Clinton, "One of the highlights of [Luckovich's] career was riding on Air Force One with U.S. President Bill Clinton in September 1996. He asked the president to draw a self-portrait, which Clinton gamely provided. 'I understood why he was trying to keep his day job,' Luckovich says."

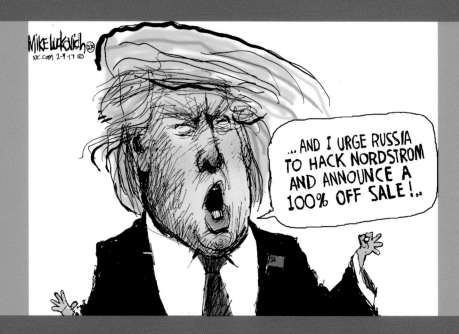

18

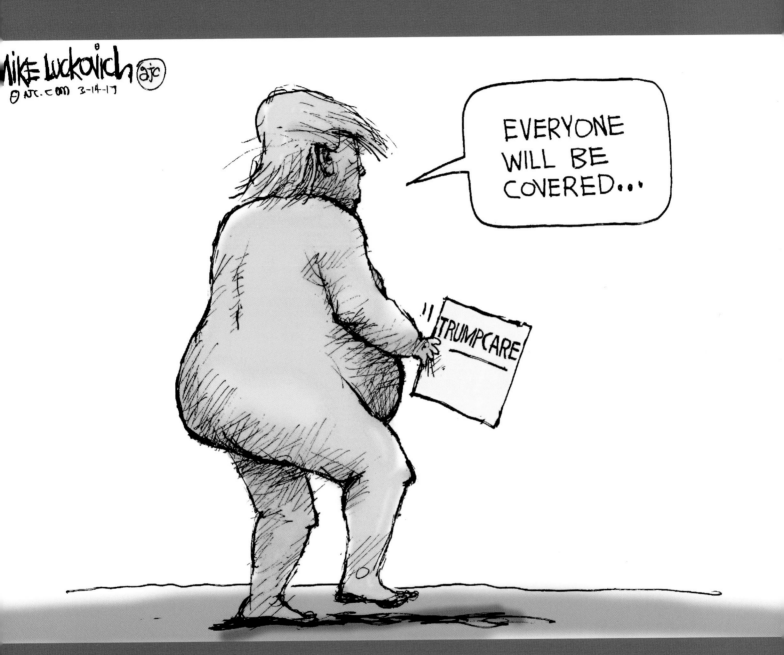

RJ Matson

Robert John Matson, born in Chicago in 1963, was raised in Brussels, Belgium and Minneapolis, Minnesota. He received a B.A. from Columbia University in 1985 and won a National Scholastic Press Association Award for cartoons he contributed to the *Columbia Daily Spectator*. Matson was also a visiting student at Pembroke College, Oxford University for one year. Matson was the editorial cartoonist at the *St. Louis Post Dispatch* from July 2005 through July 2012, the editorial cartoonist at the *New York Observer* from 1989 to 2010, and has been the editorial cartoonist and staff illustrator at *Roll Call* since 1986. His cartoons and illustrations have appeared in many other publications, including the *New Yorker*, the *Nation*, *MAD Magazine*, *City Limits*, the *Daily News*, the *Washington Post*, the *Washington City Paper*, *Capital Style*, and *Ethisphere*. His cartoons are syndicated worldwide by Cagle Cartoons.

Matson's editorial cartoons have won two Maryland-Delaware-D.C. Press Association awards and two Missouri Press Association awards. He drew *Time* magazine's Best Cartoon of the Year in 2007.

He now lives in Falmouth, Maine with his wife, Mari, and their three children.

"PUT HIM DOWN FOR TRUMP."

UNREGULATED EMISSIONS

Signe Wilkinson

Signe Wilkinson is a Pulitzer Prize-winning editorial cartoonist with the *Philadelphia Daily News* and the *Philadelphia Inquirer*. After her art training at the Pennsylvania Academy of Fine Arts, she began her career at the *San Jose Mercury News* in 1982. She moved to the *Philadelphia Daily News* in 1985 and the *Philadelphia Inquirer* in 2012. She served as president of the Association of Editorial Cartoonists in 1994. Her comic strip, *Family Tree*, ran 2008–2011. From 2011 through 2015, she drew a *Sunday Philadelphia Inquirer* comic strip called *Penn's Place*. Her books include *Abortion Cartoons on Demand*, (1992) and *One Nation, Under Surveillance*, (2005). Her work has been reprinted widely, including in the 2008 Hachette/Twelve collection: *Sex and Sensibility: Ten Women Examine the Lunacy of Modern Love in 200 Cartoons* and her 1999 Rizzolli calendar, *How to Grow the $735 Tomato*.

In addition to the Pulitzer Prize, two Robert F. Kennedy Awards and four Overseas Press Club Thomas Nast Awards, Wilkinson was named "The Pennsylvania Vegetable Substitute." She has spoken across the country about cartooning and free speech, including at an Intelligence Squared 2006 debate, *Freedom of Speech Includes the Right to Offend.*

Wilkinson lives in Philadelphia with her husband and dog "Toony."

"HAVE YOU EVER SEEN SUCH CROWDS, YOUR MAJESTY?"

Pat Byrnes

Since 1998, Pat Byrnes has been a regular contributor to the *New Yorker*. He is also a staple in *Reader's Digest*, the *Wall Street Journal*, *Barron's*, and *America* magazine. For three years, he created the syndicated comic strip *Monkeyhouse*. He has won one National Cartoonists Society "Silver Reuben" Award for advertising illustration (out of ten nominations in various categories, including five for Best Gag Cartoonist).

His gag cartoons appear in book form in *What Would Satan Do?* (Harry N. Abrams, 2005) and *Because I'm the Child Here and I Said So* (Andrews-McMeel, 2006). He illustrated *Eats Shoots & Leaves, Illustrated Edition* by Lynne Truss (Gotham 2008). He wrote and illustrated *Captain Dad: The Manly Art of Stay-at-Home Parenting* (Lyons Press, 2013) and the Captain Dad blog, praised by the *New York Times* as, "part Dave Barry, part Erma Bombeck, and all Pat Byrnes, illustrator, cartoonist, and social commentator."

He is married to Lisa Madigan, who, in addition to being brilliant and charming, is also the Attorney General of the state of Illinois. They live a surprisingly quiet life with their delightful daughters, Rebecca and Lucy, on the banks of the Chicago River.

"YOU FOOLS! IT'S GETTING AWAY."

"OR, AS WE LIKE TO CALL IT, ALTERNATIVE HEAVEN."

P. BYRNES

David Rowe

David Rowe was born in Holland and moved to Australia at the age of five. Rowe attended the Australian National University, where he studied political science and art history, and TAFE for graphic design. He attended the National School of Art in Canberra (1989–1990) before finding work at the *Canberra Times* as an illustrator (1991–1993).

For the past twenty five years, he has been employed at the *Australian Financial Review* as daily editorial cartoonist and illustrator.

Rowe is a singular practitioner of the art. He creates four to five political cartoons per week and does so with watercolors, bold brush strokes and a biting wit.

As a child, Rowe devoured the books of political cartoons his father would leave in the back of the family Volkswagen. "My parents always remember me drawing. That's all I did. I just loved caricatures and I sort of had an awareness of who the politicians (Australian) were at a very young age."

Rowe is a member of the Association for Writers and Illustrators.

PROPHECY...

HORSEY
©2016
LOS ANGELES TIMES

"As democracy is perfected, the office of the president represents, more and more closely, the inner soul of the people. On some great and glorious day, the plain folks of the land will reach their heart's desire at last, and the white house will be occupied by a downright fool and complete narcissistic moron."

—H.L. MENCKEN
THE BALTIMORE EVENING SUN
JULY 26, 1920

David Horsey

Two-time Pulitzer Prize-winning cartoonist and columnist David Horsey is a political commentator for the *Los Angeles Times.* Syndicated nationwide, David's work has appeared in hundreds of media outlets, including the *New York Times,* the *Washington Post, USA Today, Politico* and MSNBC.com.

Horsey won Pulitzers in 1999 and 2003 for cartoons published in the *Seattle Post-Intelligencer.* He received a Robert F. Kennedy Journalism Award in 2014 for his cartoons on social justice issues drawn for the *Los Angeles Times.* Horsey's other honors include the National Press Foundation's 1998 Berryman Award for cartoonist of the year and first place in the Best of the West Journalism Competition for his columns about the 2008 presidential campaign.

Horsey received a B.A. in Communications from the University of Washington in Seattle and, as a Rotary Foundation Scholar, earned an M.A. in International Relations from the University of Kent in Canterbury, England. Horsey's journalism career has taken him to national political party conventions, presidential primaries, debates and inaugurations, the Olympic Games, the Super Bowl, assignments in Europe, Japan, and Mexico, and two extended stints working at the Hearst Newspapers Washington Bureau.

He has published nine books of cartoons.

• A FUTURE TO BE AVOIDED •

John Darkow

John Darkow is an award-winning professional cartoonist. He is a native of Columbia, Michigan and an alumnus of both Rock Bridge High School and the University of Missouri. He has been a cartoonist for the *Missouri Times*, the *San Antonio Light*, the *San Antonio Current*, and, for the past ten years, the *Columbia Daily Tribune*. His cartoons are nationally syndicated by Cagle Cartoons. His cartoons have appeared in the *Times Magazine*, *Newsweek*, the *New York Times*, *Meet the Press*, CBS News, and in several books. His work is noted for his use of traditional pen and ink crosshatching and his award-winning cartoons have been published in newspapers, magazines, and books in the United States, Japan, and Europe. Darkow also works as a professional watercolorist.

He is a two-time winner of the Missouri Press Association best cartoon of the year. Darkow is particularly proud of a poster he created for the 1997 Texas Folklife Festival.

Darkow also received a perfect attendance award in the ninth grade. He is an avid bicyclist, hiker, and friend of small animals. He lives in Columbia, Missouri with his family.

Gerald Scarfe

Gerald Scarfe was born in London. He was asthmatic as a child and spent much time drawing and reading. After a brief period at the Royal College of Art in London, he established himself as a satirical cartoonist, working for *Punch* magazine and *Private Eye* during the early sixties. He was political cartoonist for the *London Sunday Times* for fifty years and worked for the *New Yorker* magazine for twenty years. His work regularly appears in many periodicals in the United Kingdom and abroad.

Scarfe has had many exhibitions worldwide, including New York, Osaka, Montreal, Los Angeles, Sydney, Melbourne, Chicago, Hanover, and London. He has had more than fifty one-man shows. He has designed the sets and costumes for plays, operas, and musicals in London, Houston, Los Angeles, San Francisco, Seattle, and New Zealand. *The Magic Flute*, designed by Scarfe, has been performed in Los Angeles, San Francisco, and Seattle. His film work includes designing and directing the animation for Pink Floyd's *The Wall*, and he was production designer on Walt Disney's animated feature film *Hercules*. Scarfe has published many books of his work.

Scarfe was made a Commander of the Most Excellent Order of the British Empire (CBE) in the 2008 Queen's Birthday Honours. He has also received Honorary Degrees from the University of Dundee and University of Kent. He is an Honorary Professor of the University of Dundee, an Honorary Fellow of the London Institute, and has received an Honorary Doctorate from the University of San Francisco. He has been a member of the Royal Designers for Industry since 1989.

Scarfe regularly gives illustrated talks about his life and work in the United Kingdom and around the world.

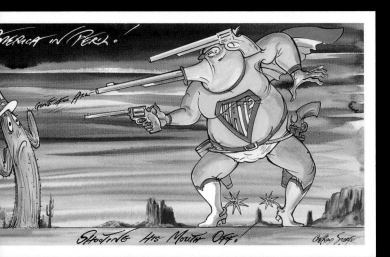

I SWEAR BY ALMIGHTY PUTIN
THAT WE WILL BUILD THOSE WALLS
BAN MUSLIMS AND SYRIAN REFUGEES
BOMB THE HELL OUT OF ISIS
IGNORE CLIMATE CHANGE
BUT TREAT PUSSY WITH RESPECT!
NOBODY'S GOING TO MESS WITH US
WE'RE GOING TO MAKE AMERICA
HATE AGAIN!!!

Marian Kamensky

Marian Kamensky was born on April 1, 1957 in Levoca, Slovakia. He was twelve years old when his parents moved to the village of Hrachovo where he started drawing. After finishing school, he worked as a glassblower in Poltar. Two years later, he moved to Prague, Czech Republic, where he worked as a property master at the famous Vinohrady Theater. In 1981, Kamensky moved to Hamburg, Germany, where he studied Lithography at the Hamburg Arts College. In 1982, he began illustrating the satirical books of Gabriel Laub. He also created illustrations for adventure books by Rudiger Nehberg and the biology/zoology literature of Christian Kuehl. For a number of years, his artworks were published in newspapers and magazines in European countries including, *Die Zeit*, *Der Spiegel*, *Focus*, *Nebelspalter*, *Eulenspiegel*, and *Psychologie Heute*. He also published work in the United States and Canada in *Playboy*, the *New York Sun*, the *Humanist*, and others. In 2001, he returned to Slovakia where he lived and worked in Rimavská Sobota. His artworks were presented at exhibitions including, Galerie Schnecke in Hamburg, Galerie Futurum in Hamburg, Galerie Dobach in Wurselem, Galerie Artica in Cuxhaven, Galerie Stein in Gelsenkirchen, Galerie "das auge" in Lauda, and Galerie Vita in Switzerland.

In 2010, Kamensky moved to Austria, where he lives in Vienna and continues his creative work as an illustrator and cartoonist.

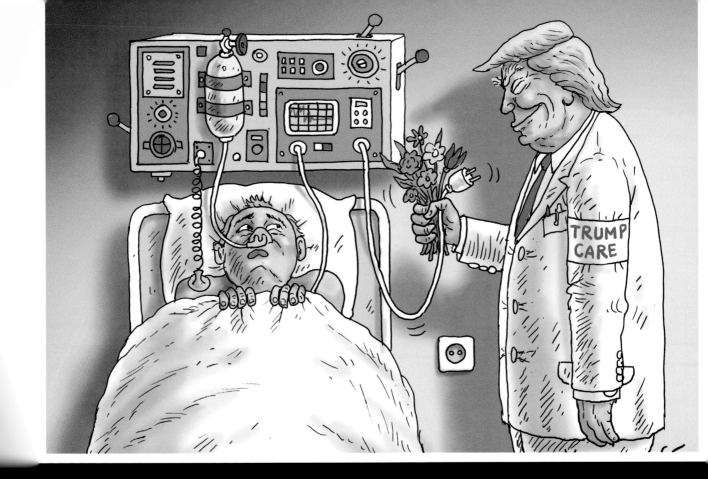

Daryl Cagle

For the past thirty-five years, Daryl Cagle has been one of America's most prolific cartoonists. He worked for fifteen years with Jim Henson's *Muppets*, illustrating scores of books, magazines, calendars, and products. Cagle still sees pigs, frogs, *Sesame Street*, and *Fraggle Rock* characters when he closes his eyes.

Cagle worked for many years as an advertising illustrator, doing cartoon campaigns for such clients as Discover Card, McDonalds, Sega, and General Foods Post Cereals. He drew a syndicated comic called *True!* in the 1990's for Tribune Media Services. He worked as the editorial cartoonist in Hawaii, and drew for the *Washington Post's* Slate.com site before working seven years as the cartoonist for MSNBC.com. In 2001, Cagle started a new syndicate, Cagle Cartoons, Inc., which distributes the cartoons of sixty editorial cartoonists and fourteen columnists to more than 1,000 subscribing newspapers in the United States and around the world, including over half of America's daily, paid-circulation newspapers.

Cagle is a past president of the National Cartoonists Society and the National Cartoonists Society Foundation.

50

Liza Donnelly

Liza Donnelly lives in New York and is a writer and award-winning cartoonist with the *New Yorker Magazine*. She is resident cartoonist for CBS News. Her work can also be seen in the *New York Times*, *Medium*, *Forbes*, and *Politico*.

She is the creator of a new digital visual reporting/editorial cartooning called live-drawing. Donnelly was the first cartoonist to be granted access on-location to live draw the Academy Awards; she has also live drawn the Grammys, Tonys, the 2016 Democratic Convention and more. Her innovative approach to reporting and commenting on events has been covered by CBS News, NBC News, *Ad Week*, *USA Today*, *Watch Magazine*, and *People* magazine.

Donnelly is a Cultural Envoy for the U.S. State Department, traveling the world to speak about freedom of speech and women's rights. Donnelly's TED talk, *Drawing on Humor for Change*, was translated into thirty-eight languages and viewed over one million times. She was profiled on CBS *Sunday Morning*, and has been a guest on podcasts, television, and radio shows. She has been interviewed for numerous publications. Donnelly is the recipient of an honorary Ph.D. from University of Connecticut and is the author/editor of eighteen books. She is a charter member of the international project, Cartooning for Peace.

52

Darrin Bell

Darrin Bell navigates issues such as civil rights, pop culture, family, science fiction, scriptural wisdom, and nihilist philosophy while often casting his subjects in roles that are traditionally denied them. Bell began his freelance editorial cartooning career in 1995 at the age of twenty. His first sale was to the *Los Angeles Times*, which subsequently assigned him a cartoon every other week. He also sold his cartoons to the *San Francisco Chronicle* and the former ANG papers, which included the *Oakland Tribune*. While he was a political science major at University of California, Berkeley, Bell became the editorial cartoonist for the *Daily Californian*. His work won several California Intercollegiate Press Association awards and an SPJ Mark of Excellence Award. He was a two-time runner-up for the Charles M. Schulz Award, as well as a runner-up for the Locher Award.

Muslim students protested Bell's 9/11 editorial cartoon and brought him to national attention. "Muslim-Americans were understandably fearful of being profiled and persecuted. When faced with that fear, it's inevitable that some will grossly misinterpret a cartoon," he says. "But you can't let the fear of irrational reactions—or the knowledge that many will say 'it's too soon' for anything other than comforting images—stop you from saying what you believe to be true. I believe it's never 'too soon' for candor."

Bell creates two syndicated comic strips, *Candorville* and *Rudy Park*, and is a storyboard artist. He lives in Los Angeles.

"I don't care what the CIA says, Russia had nothing to do with my election."

Pat Bagley

Pat Bagley has been the editorial cartoonist for the *Salt Lake Tribune* for thirty-two years. An acknowledged master illustrator and commentator on the comic politics of red-state Utah, Bagley's national and world cartoons have also appeared in publications such as *Time*, the *Irish Times*, the *Guardian*, the *Wall Street Journal*, the *Washington Post*, and the *Los Angeles Times*. One of the most popular syndicated cartoonists with politicalcartoons. com, Bagley has won prestigious cartooning awards, including the 2009 Herblock Award.

His 2005 book, *Clueless George Goes to War*, was lauded as one of the most radioactive critiques of President George W. Bush's decision to invade and occupy Iraq.

Bagley's familiarity with politics is in his DNA. He was born in Salt Lake City, but raised in Oceanside, California where his father worked in city government. The elder Bagley worked his way up from a draftsman in the Oceanside planning department to city manager, and then ran for mayor and successfully served three terms. Watching the evening news and reading the newspaper was a popular Bagley family activity.

Bagley served in a Latter-day Saints mission to Bolivia and later cut his teeth on cartooning at the Brigham Young University school newspaper, the *Daily Universe*. He describes himself as "Mormon Emeritus." He lives in Utah and has two sons.

WESTMINSTER DOG

"I'VE NEVER SEEN SUCH EFFORTLESS CONTROL!"

Mark Bryan

As a child of the 50s and 60s, Bryan absorbed the mixed legacy of postwar pop culture and politics: superhero comics, sci-fi books, the *Mouseketeers*, *Zap Comics*, *Mad Magazine*, the Kennedy and Martin Luther King assassinations, Tricky Dick and the Vietnam War. These influences and events, plus the "duck and cover" mentality of the Red Scare, had their shots at a sensitive mind and provoked a sense that all is not right with the human species.

Like many disenchanted boomers, he explored alternate lifestyles and alternate realities which may explain in part his affection for pop-surrealism. While attending art school at Otis Art Institute in the 70s, he worked with the Los Four (a Chicano Artists collective), who introduced him to the mural works of Rivera, Siqueiros, and Orozco, and thus the value and long tradition of political art. Over the past thirty years, Bryan has explored the serious absurdities of the human condition, including never-ending political hijinks, war, terrorism, and environmental destruction. Despite the disturbing nature of these topics, Bryan always manages to portray them with humor and insight. Bryan has exhibited his work throughout the United States, Canada, Europe, and Japan. His work appears on satirical and political web sites across the United States and internationally. It has been featured as illustration and cover art for publications, including *Juxtapoz*, *Fifth Estate*, *American Bystander* and *Adbusters* magazines.

Bryan has lived on the Central Coast of California for the past forty years and tries to paint and surf as much as possible. He has a son, a daughter, a grandson, three granddaughters and a Toyota truck.

You may see and learn more about Bryan's work at artofmarkbryan.com.

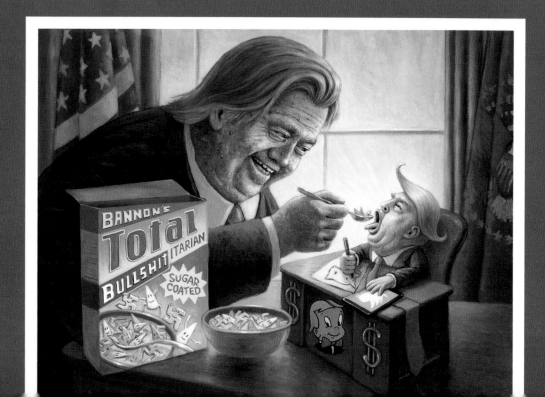

Andy Marlette

Andy Marlette is the nationally syndicated editorial cartoonist for the *Pensacola News Journal*. Born and raised by underpaid public school teachers in Sanford, Florida, Marlette received a priceless editorial cartoon education from his uncle, Pulitzer Prize-winning cartoonist Doug Marlette. The elder Marlette drew with a ferocity that left no politician revered and no hypocrite unexposed. His creed was simple; "In this country, we do not apologize for our opinions." With this in mind, Andy works daily to carry on the family tradition and to always be an "equal opportunity offender."

Marlette's cartoons are distributed throughout the United States by Creators Syndicate and the *USA Today* Network. In addition to cartooning, Marlette is also a columnist and editorial writer. His work has become both hated and adored by readers in Northwest Florida. He has been awarded by the Florida Society of Newspaper Editors for both his writing and cartoons.

Marlette resides in Pensacola, Florida with his lovely wife, Dahlonega.

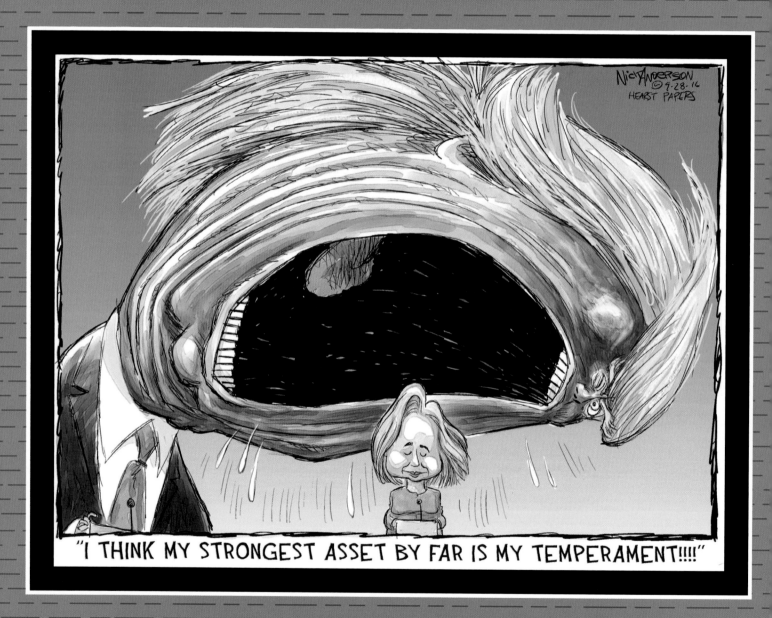

"I THINK MY STRONGEST ASSET BY FAR IS MY TEMPERAMENT!!!!"

Nick Anderson

Nick Anderson, of the *Houston Chronicle*, is an avowed independent who covers politics and contemporary cultural issues in a way that connects with readers. His loose, idiosyncratic style carries with it an unconventional message that has broad appeal. "I approach my work with a healthy skepticism for the ideological extremists littering our political landscape," explains Anderson.

In 2005, Anderson was awarded the Pulitzer Prize for Editorial Cartooning. The judges complimented his "unusual graphic style that produced extraordinarily thoughtful and powerful messages."

Anderson has pioneered a method of coloring his cartoons. Using an advanced computer program, he creates digital paintings characterized by subtle textures and striking images. Because of his innovative use of the program, its manufacturer, Corel Corporation, has designated Anderson a "Painter Master."

Anderson has worked for the *Louisville Courier-Journal* as associate editorial cartoonist and the *Houston Chronicle* as editorial cartoonist.

Steve Benson

When Steve Benson was a young boy producing the crayon doodlings that eventually led him into a career as a professional cartoonist, his mother gave him some advice. "Stephen," she said, "you can catch a lot more flies with honey than you can with vinegar." Steve replied, "Yeah, Mom, but who wants more flies?" From behind his drawing board at the *Arizona Republic*, editorial "harpoonist" Steve Benson regularly lobs his ink-bottle grenades, drawing beads on rascals in high places, as well as drawing fire.

In 1993, Benson won the Pulitzer Prize for editorial cartooning. His cartoons have also earned him a National Headliner Award, an Overseas Press Club Citation for Excellence, a Rocky Mountain Emmy, a place in Who's Who in the West, and several Best of the West and Arizona Press Club Awards. He was a 2002 recipient of the American Civil Liberties Union "Practitioner of the First Amendment Award." In 2014, he won the Sigma Delta Chi Award for editorial cartooning.

His cartoons are nationally distributed by Creators Syndicate. They have also appeared in *Time*, *Newsweek*, *U.S. News & World Report*, the *New York Times*, and the *Washington Post*, as well as on CNN, MSNBC, ABC's *Nightline*, CBS's *60 Minutes*, and PBS's *Mac-Neil-Lehrer Report*. Steve is the author of five books of his editorial cartoons.

Steve and his wife, Mary Ann Christensen, live in Gilbert, Arizona with their four children.

Michael Ramirez

Two-time Pulitzer Prize-winner Michael Ramirez combines an encyclopedic knowledge of the news with a captivating drawing style to create consistently outstanding editorial cartoons. Ramirez, who studied pre-med at the University of California, Irvine, originally considered journalism a hobby, but he was hooked when his first cartoon for the college newspaper, lampooning candidates for student office, had the student assembly demanding an apology. "Editorial cartoons should be smart and substantive, provocative and informative. They should stir passions and deep emotions. Editorial cartoons should be a catalyst for thought, and, frankly speaking, if you can make politicians think, that is an accomplishment in itself… If I don't get at least one death threat every few months, then I am not doing my job," Ramirez says of his penchant for speaking controversy.

In addition to the 1994 and 2008 Pulitzer Prizes, Ramirez was the 2008 winner of the prestigious Fischetti Award. He is a three-time Sigma Delta Chi, Society of Professional Journalism Award winner, a Lincoln Fellow, and a recipient of the UCI Medal.

He was formerly the editorial cartoonist for the *Los Angeles Times*, the *Memphis Commercial Appeal*, *Investor's Business Daily*, and a contributing cartoonist for *USA Today*.

His work is syndicated by Creators Syndicate.

Steve Breen

Two-time Pulitzer Prize-winner Steve Breen is has developed a reputation for provocative political cartoons that have captured the attention of some of the nation's premier publications. A southern California native, Breen spent much of his childhood at home reading *Mad Magazine* while his friends were off at the beach. Although he earned a degree in political science and a U.S. history teaching credential, Breen was hooked on cartooning as a career after one of his cartoons was published in *Newsweek* when he was only nineteen years old.

He won the John Locher and Charles M. Schulz cartooning awards for his work on the student newspaper at the University of California at Riverside. Breen has been an editorial cartoonist at the *San Diego Union-Tribune* since July 2001. Prior to that, he was at New Jersey's *Asbury Park Press*. He is the winner of the 2007 Berryman Award presented by the National Press Foundation, and the 1998 and 2009 Pulitzer Prize for Editorial Cartooning. Steve's editorial cartoons are nationally syndicated by Creators Syndicate and appear regularly in the *New York Times*, *USA Today*, *Newsweek*, and *U.S. News & World Report*.

He is the author and illustrator of three children's books: *Stick*, *Violet the Pilot*, and *The Secret of Santa's Island*.

Steve Sack

Steve Sack was born in Saint Paul, Minnesota. His newspaper career began while attending the University of Minnesota where he illustrated features and drew editorial cartoons for the school paper, the *Minnesota Daily*. Two years later, he was hired as staff cartoonist for the *Journal Gazette* in Fort Wayne, Indiana. He is currently an editorial cartoonist working for the *Star Tribune* in Minneapolis and has been with the paper since 1981. With Chris Foote, he draws the cartoon activity panel *Doodles*. In addition to cartoons, Sack is a master at oil painting and has had many gallery exhibits of his work. Sack's cartooning work is unique in that he draws his entire cartoons on an iPad.

Sack won the Pulitzer Prize in 2013 for editorial cartooning. In addition, Sack has won multiple awards during his career which include, The Cliffors K. and James T. Berryman Award, awarded annually by the National Press Foundation for the nation's best editorial cartoonist (2006), The Scripps Howard Foundation, National Journalism Award (2004), and the National Headliner Award (2003).

His editorial cartoons are distributed by Cagle Cartoons.

Bob Englehart

Bob Englehart, born November 7, 1945, is the first full-time editorial cartoonist in the history of the oldest newspaper in America, the *Hartford Courant*, and has been with the paper since 1980. He previously worked at *Chicago American Today* from 1967 to 1972, the *Journal-Gazette* in Fort Wayne, Indiana from 1973 to 1975, and the Dayton, Ohio *Journal Herald* from 1975 to 1980.

Englehart has won awards from the U.N. Population Institute, H.L. Mencken Award, and Planned Parenthood. Bob was the sole nominee for the Pulitzer Prize in 1980.

His work is collected by the Ohio State Cartoon Library, Indiana University-Purdue University Library in Fort Wayne, Connecticut Historical Society, Eastern Connecticut State University, and the University of Connecticut.

Englehart lives in Middletown, Connecticut with his wife, Pat McGrath. Together they have three grown children and two grandchildren.

The CREATION...

Adam Zyglis

Adam Zyglis, originally from Buffalo, New York, is the Pulitzer Prize-winning editorial cartoonist for the *Buffalo News*. In 2004, he graduated from the Canisius College Honors program *summa cum laude*, with a major in Computer Science, a minor in Math, and a concentration in Studio Arts. Zyglis's first cartooning job was for the *Griffin*, the weekly student newspaper at the college. Because of his work at the newspaper in 2003, he was honored with a first place national award from the Associated Collegiate Press and the Universal Press Syndicate. He placed second in the 2004 John Locher Memorial Award and he was a finalist in the 2003 Charles M. Schultz Award. As a senior, he wrote his honors thesis on the art of editorial cartooning. He met many inspiring people at Canisius, including his wife, Jessica. His cartoons are internationally syndicated and have appeared in many publications around the world, including the *Washington Post, USA Today*, the *New York Times* and the *Los Angeles Times*. In his spare time, he has done freelance work in book illustration and storyboarding. His work has also appeared magazines such as the *Week, Time*, and *MAD Magazine*.

In 2013, he won the Clifford K. and James T. Berryman Award, given by the National Press Foundation. In 2007, 2011 and 2015 he won a National Headliner Award sponsored by the Atlantic City Press Club. Additionally, he was awarded the Grambs Aronson Cartooning with a Conscience award and the Pulitzer Prize in 2015.

MORIN

Miami Herald

Jim Morin

Born in Washington, D.C. and raised outside of Boston, Massachusetts, Jim Morin started drawing cartoons at age seven. Fueled by social and political upheavals during the early 1970s, he began publishing political cartoons in his Syracuse University paper, the *Daily Orange*. Morin joined the staff at the *Miami Herald* in 1978. Morin shared a Pulitzer with other members of the *Miami Herald* editorial board in 1983 and was a finalist for the prize in 1977 and 1990. Morin won the Pulitzer Prize for editorial cartooning in 1996 and 2017. In 1996, Morin won the National Press Foundation's Berryman Award. In 1999, he won the Thomas Nast Society Award. He won the John Fischetti Award in 2000, the Herblock Prize in 2007, and others.

His work has been published in numerous collections, including *Line of Fire*, *AmBUSHED*, and *Jim Morin's World*. Other books include *Jim Morin's Field Guide to Birds* and *Famous Cats*. He is also a passionate oil and watercolor painter. His work has been exhibited in galleries and museums throughout south Florida.

Morin's work is syndicated internationally by MorinToons Syndicate.

TRUMP CARE

05-13-17
MORIN

MorinToons Syndicate

Steve Brodner

Steve Brodner is a leading political caricaturist and satiric commentator in the United States. His work has appeared in most major publications since the 1970's. He has been a regular contributor to the *New Yorker*, the *Nation*, the *New York Times*, the *Los Angeles Times*, *Esquire*, and *Spy*.

His career as an art journalist has led him to cover twelve national political conventions, the Farm Crisis of the 1980's, the Bob Dole Campaign of 1996, a climb up Mt. Fuji, and to Samsø Island, the world's first green energy community, in Denmark.

Brodner has won most of the major awards in the graphic arts industry, including medals at the Society of Illustrators, American Illustration, Communication Arts, Hunter College's Aronson Medal for Social Justice Journalism, Cooper Union's St. Gardens Medal, etc.

He teaches art at the School of Visual Arts in New York.

Phil Hands

Phil Hands, born Oct. 30, 1980, in Syracuse, New York, is an American editorial cartoonist best known for his work at the *Wisconsin State Journal* in Madison, Wisconsin.

Hands grew up in the Detroit area before moving to Wisconsin in 2005. He is a graduate of Kenyon College in Gambier, Ohio and received his master's degree from the University of Wisconsin-Madison.

Hands began drawing cartoons for the *State Journal* as an intern in 2004 and became a regular freelancer in 2005. He joined the staff of the *State Journal* in 2013 and is currently the only cartoonist on the staff of a newspaper in Wisconsin. His cartoons have appeared in *USA Today*, *Newsweek*, *Time*, and the *Washington Post*.

Hands has won a number of state and national awards for editorial cartooning and was the 2012 recipient of the Society of Professional Journalists Sigma Delta Chi award for editorial cartooning.

He lives in Madison with his very understanding wife, Tricia, and his two adorable children, Owen and Claire. In his spare time he enjoys drinking coffee, eating cheese, and being cold. His cartoons are syndicated nationally by the Tribune Content Agency.

WISCONSIN STATE

OBA

Michael de Adder

Michael de Adder was born in Moncton, New Brunswick, Canada. He studied art at Mount Allison University where he received a Bachelor of Fine Arts in drawing and painting. De Adder freelances for the *Halifax Chronicle Herald*, the *Toronto Star*, and *Ottawa Hill Times*. De Adder reaches millions of readers per week, making him one of the most read cartoonists in Canada. He is also the author of seven books.

Michael has received the following awards: Atlantic Journalism Award for Editorial Cartooning (2001), Atlantic Journalism Award for Editorial Cartooning (2002), National Newspaper Award, Citation of Merit (2002), Atlantic Journalism Award for Editorial Cartooning (2006), American Association of Editorial Cartoonists Golden Spike Award (2006), Atlantic Journalism Award—Gold Innovation Award (for CBC animations) (2008), Atlantic Journalism Award for Editorial Cartooning(2009), and Atlantic Journalism Award for Editorial cartooning(2011).

His work is syndicated throughout North America by artizans.com.de.

Rainer Hachfeld

Born in Ludwigshafen in 1939, Rainer Hachfeld is a German playwright and political cartoonist. Having studied art in Berlin, he began his career as a caricaturist in *Spandauer Volksblatt* in 1966, and then in *EXTRA-Blatt*. He has also contributed to *Stern* and *Der Abend*. Since 1990, he has worked with the socialist daily *Neues Deutschland*.

Selected books include, *Der Struwwelpeter neu frisiert* (with his father and copywriter Eckart Hachfeld) (1969), *Marx and Maoritz* (Klaus Budzinsky) (1970), *Yankee Go Home* (1971), *Rattenbuch* (with texts by Martin Buchholz) (1975), *Bananen & Kanonen* (1979, Swedish edition 1984), *The IGMetall, small picture story of a large trade union* (1991), *The GRIPS-Liederbuch* (Texts: V. Ludwig, B. Heymann) (1999), and *Rat, Bär & Co, 100 Berlin Caricatures from 40 Years* (2009).

Hachfeld's cartoons can be found in numerous contributions to anthologies and catalogs.

His work is available in North America through Cagle Cartoons Syndicate.

Dave Granlund

National cartoonist Dave Granlund's blog features his take on politics and current events. He has been an editorial cartoonist in daily newspapers since 1977. Born in Ware, Massachusetts, Granlund began drawing cartoons in grade school. He was published on the editorial pages of local weekly newspapers at age sixteen.

His eight-year enlistment in the United States Air Force included assignments with Strategic Air Command and with Headquarters Command, where his duties included work as head illustrator for the Presidential Inaugural Subcommittee, providing briefing charts for the White House, and support for Air Force One. As part of NATO in Operation Looking Glass with the Airborne Command Post, he was awarded the Joint Service Commendation Medal.

Granlund's newspaper honors include awards from UPI, New England Press Association, International Association of Business Communicators, The Associated Press and Massachusetts Press Association.

His work is currently syndicated by Cagle Cartoons.

Ann Telnaes

Ann Telnaes creates editorial cartoons in various mediums, including animation, visual essays, live sketches, and traditional print for the *Washington Post*. Telnaes attended California Institute of the Arts and graduated with a Bachelor of Fine Arts. Before beginning her career as an editorial cartoonist, Telnaes worked for several years as a designer for Walt Disney Imagineering. She has also animated and designed for various studios in Los Angeles, New York, London, and Taiwan. She has appeared on *The Newshour with Jim Lehrer*, C-Span, NPR, BBC radio, Sirius XM Radio, and *The Editors*, World Affairs Television, Canada.

She won the Pulitzer Prize in 2001 for her print cartoons and the National Cartoonists Society's Reuben for Outstanding Cartoonist of the Year for 2016. Telnaes' print work was shown in a solo exhibition at the Great Hall in the Thomas Jefferson Building of the Library of Congress in 2004. Other awards include: The National Cartoonists Society Reuben division award for Editorial Cartoons (2016), The National Press Foundation's Berryman Award (2006), The Maggie Award, Planned Parenthood (2002), Fifteenth Annual International Dutch Cartoon Festival (2007), The National Headliner Award (1997), The Population Institute XVII Global Media Awards (1996), Sixth Annual Environmental Media Awards (1996).

Her first book, *Humor's Edge*, was published by Pomegranate Press and the Library of Congress in 2004. A collection of Vice President Cheney cartoons, *Dick*, was self-published by Telnaes and Sara Thaves in 2006. Her work has also been exhibited in Paris, Jerusalem, and Lisbon.

ANNTELNAES 1/21/17

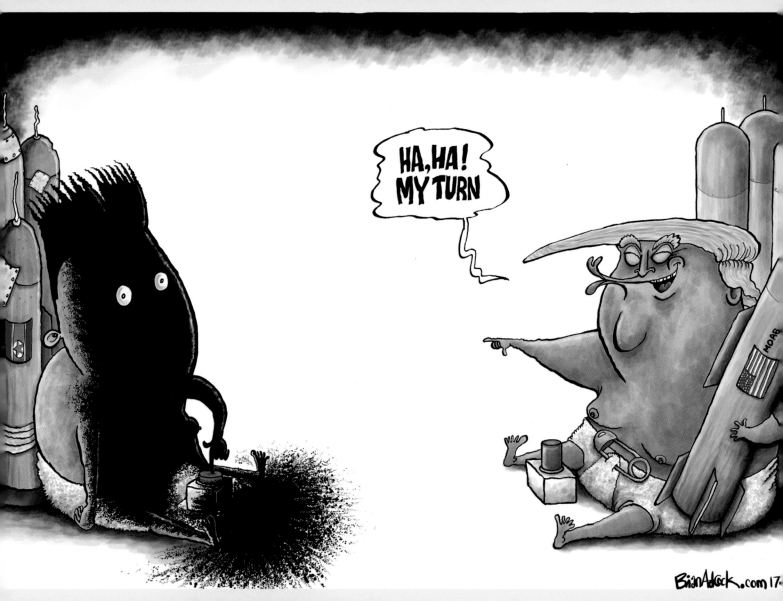

Brian Adcock

Brian Adcock was born in Scotland. He became a professional illustrator/political cartoonist in 2000, when he started supplying cartoons for the *Prague Post* while living in the Czech Republic.

On returning to the United Kingdom, Brian continued to work for the *Prague Post*, as well as supplying his local paper with *TILT*, an off-the-wall cartoon series. Shortly after that, he began drawing political cartoons for *Scotland on Sunday*, the *Scotsman* and the *Edinburgh Evening News*. He works regularly for the *Independent* and has supplied cartoons for the *Guardian*, *Teaching Scotland*, and various other publications. He has also illustrated the children's book *Cinnamon and the Bat People*.

He has supplied illustrations for various museums such as the Time and Tide Museum in Great Yarmouth, the Ancient House Museum in Thetford, and the Bridewell Museum in Norwich.

His editorial cartoons are syndicated in North America by Cagle Cartoons.

117

THE DUNCE WALK...

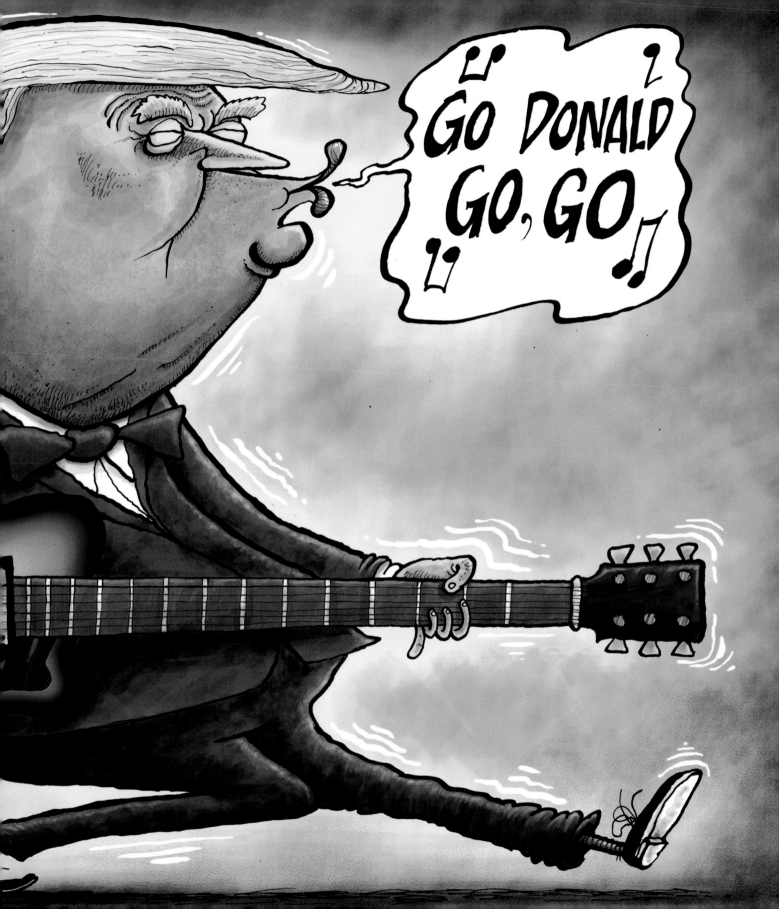

Kevin Siers

Pulitzer Prize-winning cartoonist Kevin Siers creates five editorial cartoons each week for the *Charlotte Observer*. A native of Minnesota, he has been drawing for the *Observer* since 1987.

He began his cartooning career drawing editorial cartoons for his hometown community newspaper between shifts working in the local iron ore mines north of Duluth. While attending the University of Minnesota, he joined the staff of the *Minnesota Daily* as editorial cartoonist. There, his work won top national awards for student cartoonists, including The Sigma Delta Chi / Society of Professional Journalists Award and the John Locher Memorial Award, sponsored by the American Association of Editorial Cartoonists. His work for the *Charlotte Observer* was awarded the Pulitzer Prize for editorial cartooning in 2014. Siers has also been published in the *New York Times*, the *Washington Post*, *Newsweek*, and *USA Today*.

Other artistic pursuits include singing tenor in the Charlotte choral group Renaissance, and mastering fly-fishing techniques, which he practices on North Carolina mountain trout every chance he gets. He and his wife live in Charlotte, North Carolina.

His cartoons are distributed nationwide by King Features Syndicate.

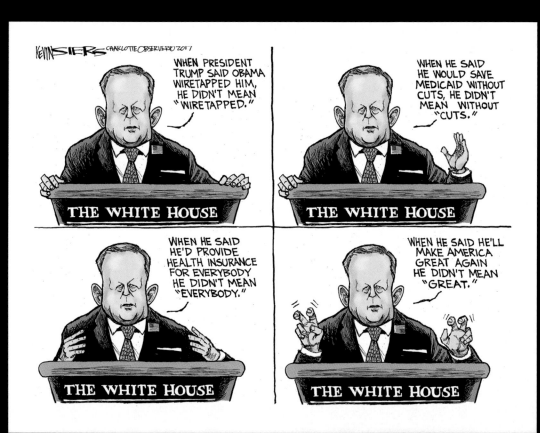

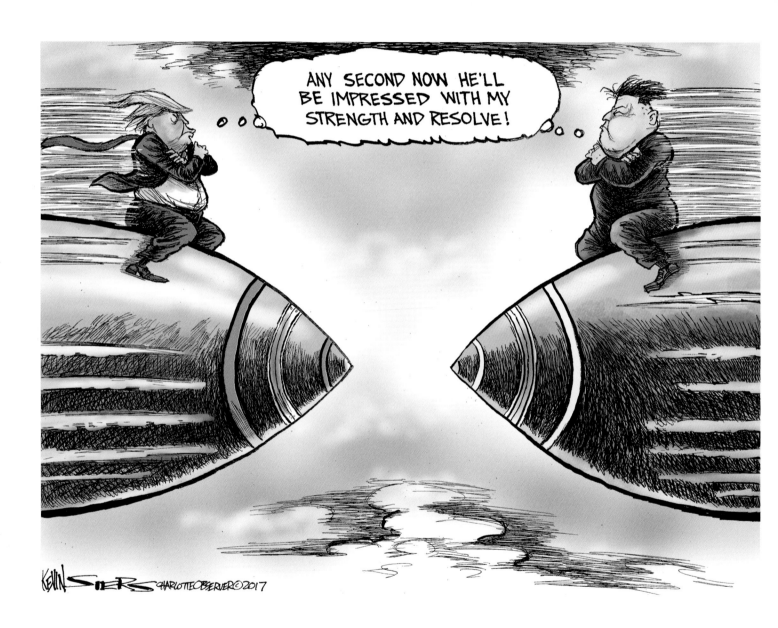

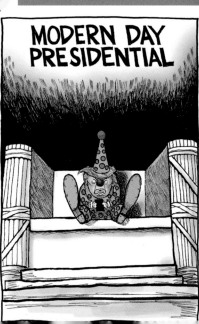

Donald Trump's Gettysburg Address

Tom Stiglich

Cartooning is Tom's life. He started as a child and has not stopped. Born and raised in Philadelphia, drawing has been a great way to support a serious cheesesteak addiction.

His cartoons appear in *USA Today*, the *New York Times*, *Newsweek*, *Newsweek Japan*, TIME.com, the *Philadelphia Inquirer*, the *Philadelphia Daily News*, the *Chicago Sun-Times*, the *Los Angeles Times*, the *Hawaii Tribune Herald*, and the annual book series *Best Editorial Cartoons of the Year*.

He has received four citation of Excellence Ranan Lurie awards from the United Nations, numerous awards with the Greater Philadelphia Society of Journalists, and currently has cartoons on exhibit at the Charles M. Schulz museum in Santa Rosa, California.

His greatest honor to date is spending time visiting with troops in Kuwait, Iraq, Turkey, Kosovo and Germany through the NCS and USO.

Stiglich is a member of the National Cartoonists Society and the Association of American Editorial Cartoonists. His editorial cartoons are nationally syndicated by Creators Syndicate and can be seen regularly in over 300 newspapers throughout the United States.

Matt Wuerker

Matt Wuerker is the staff cartoonist for *Politico*. As part of the team that launched *Politico* in 2006, he provides editorial cartoons, illustrations, caricatures, and web animations for both the print and web platforms of the publication.

Over the past forty years, Wuerker's cartoons have been used widely in publications that range from dailies like the *Los Angeles Times*, the *Washington Post*, and the *Christian Science Monitor* to magazines such as *Newsweek*, the *Nation*, and *Smithsonian*—to name a few.

He won the Pulitzer Prize in 2012. In 2010, he was awarded the Herblock Prize at the Library of Congress and later that year won the National Press Foundation's Berryman Award.

Wuerker has published two collections of cartoons, *Standing Tall in Deep Doo Doo, A Cartoon Chronicle of the Bush/Quayle Years* (Thunder's Mouth Press, 1991) and *Meanwhile in Other News… A Graphic Look at Politics in the Empire of Money, Sex and Scandal* (Common Courage Press, 1998). He illustrated the book *The Madness of King George* (Common Courage Press, 2003) by Michael K. Smith.

M.WUERKER
POLITICO   Andrew McMeel

Andrew Rae

Andrew Rae is an illustrator and member of the multi-disciplinary Peepshow Collective. He uses simple, hand rendered line and a combination of paper, felt pens, watercolor, iPad, iMac, and Wacom pads and screens to render irreverent images of characters, ghouls, robots, machines, and creatures which are used in an editorial, publishing, advertising, animation, and mural context.

Rae is a regular contributor to the *New York Times Magazine* and has worked for many clients worldwide, including the London Science Museum, Google, and the *Guardian*. He was art director on the award-winning BBC animation *Monkey Dust*.

His graphic novel, *Moonhead and the Music Machine*, is published by Nobrow. Rae illustrated *This is Warhol*, *This is Dali*, *Where's Warhol*, and *My Crazy Inventions Sketchbook* published by Laurence King.

He lives and works in London, near Highgate Cemetery.

This Town Melts Down

At large in Trump's Washington.

By Mark Leibovich
Illustrations by Andrew Rae

Olle Magnusson

Olle Magnusson, born 1962, is a Swedish cartoonist, illustrator, and art director. In 1982, Magnusson started working as editorial cartoonist for a number of Swedish newspapers including, the *Östgöta Correspondenten*. He also did illustrations for Företagarförbundet, an association of small business owners. In 1990, Magnusson began working in the advertising business as an art director while also continuing his work in illustration. He was a guest speaker at EuroCature 2016 in Vienna, Austria.

The blog at www.oddonkey.com featured Magnusson in their interview series on March 7, 2014. The article said of Magnusson, "His caricatures truly are little precious masterpieces. What is most striking is Magnusson's extraordinary precision in grasping the likeness of his subject while maintaining an immediately recognizable style… Magnusson knows exactly where to go and when to stop before losing the likeness."

Magnusson's editorial cartoon work is world syndicated via Tribune News Service, Bulls Press and Newsmap.

His blog is http://karikatyrer-ollemagnusson.blogspot.com/.

Nate Beeler

Nate Beeler's cartooning career began at his high school's student newspaper in Columbus, Ohio. He went on to earn a journalism degree at American University in 2002. Beeler won the three major college cartooning awards: the Charles M. Schulz Award, the John Locher Award and the SPJ Mark of Excellence Award.

He is the editorial cartoonist for the *Columbus Dispatch*. Prior to joining the *Dispatch*, he was the cartoonist for the *Washington Examiner* from 2005 to 2012. His award-winning cartoons have appeared on CNN, Fox News, and MSNBC, and in such publications as *Time, Newsweek, USA Today*, and the *Los Angeles Times*, among others. Beeler's cartoons are distributed internationally to more than 800 publications by Cagle Cartoons.

In 2014, Beeler won the Fischetti Award from Columbia College Chicago. He was awarded the 2010 Thomas Nast Award from the Overseas Press Club of America and the 2008 Clifford K. & James T. Berryman Award from The National Press Foundation. He has also received multiple honors from the Virginia, Maryland, and D.C. press associations for his cartoons. In 2007, he won the Golden Spike Award at the Association of American Editorial Cartoonists' 50th anniversary convention in Washington.

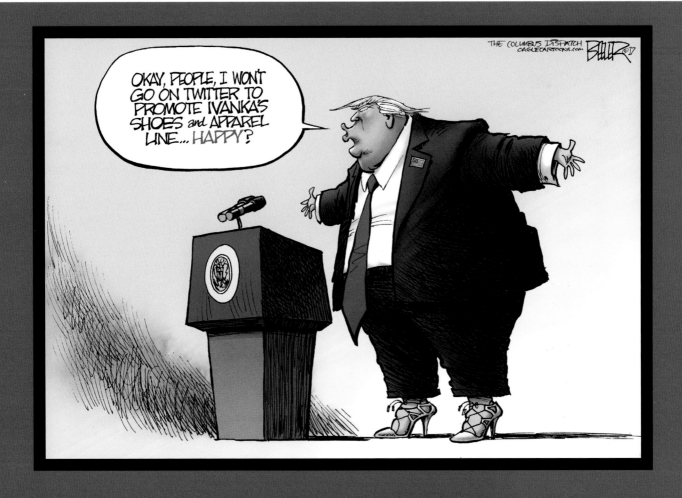

NUCLEAR BRINKMANSHIP

MAGA

THE COLUMBUS DISPATCH
CAGLECARTOONS.COM

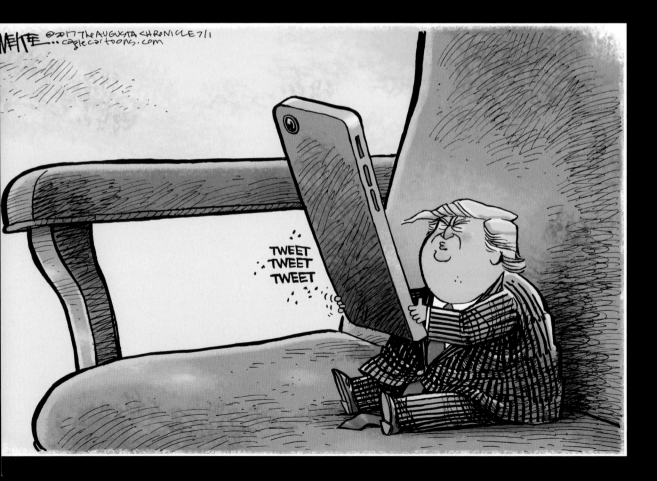

Rick McKee

Rick McKee has been editorial cartoonist for the *Augusta Chronicle* (Georgia) since 1998. His cartoons are syndicated by Cagle Cartoons to over 850 newspapers around the world. In 2013, McKee won first place in the The United Nations/Ranan Lurie Political Cartoon annual competition. The award is granted for cartoons which reflect "the spirit and the principles of the United Nations." In addition to appearing in most major American newspapers, McKee's award-winning work has been featured on CNN/Headline News, the Fox News Channel, and in *Newsweek*. A collection of his cartoons, *Painting With a Broad Brush*, was published in November 2015.

McKee, born in Florida, loved to draw at an early age. An article entitled "Cartoonists ink drawings without fear or favor" in the January 4, 1998 *Augusta Chronicle* described McKee as, "a son of the South who seems to have always had a politically feisty streak. At age 12, he fired off a letter to then-President Jimmy Carter jabbing his support for the so-called Equal Rights Amendment. The youngster received a form response 'with the usual bull,' which no doubt sharpened Rick's instincts for future dealings with politicians." In 1987, he graduated from Samford University in Birmingham, Alabama with a degree in graphic design. He was the political cartoonist for *The Samford Crimson*.

McKee's philosophy is to speak out without fear or favor—and to make readers think.

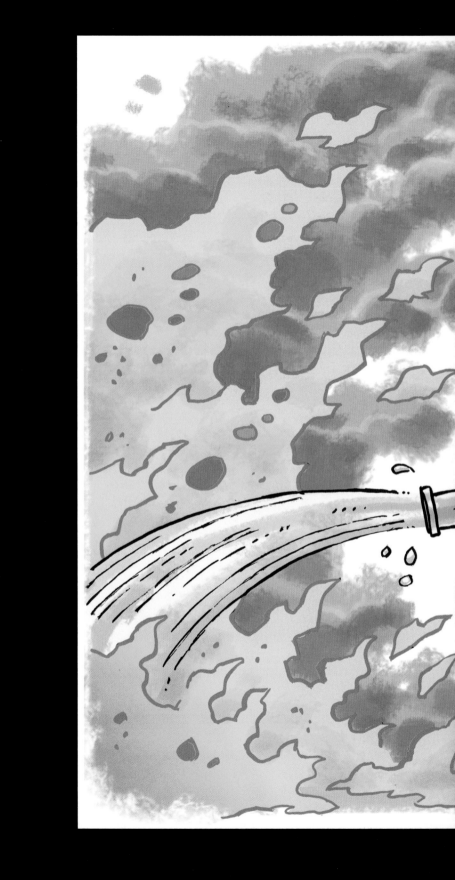

Jan-Erik Ander

Jan-Erik Ander, (born 1946) in Norrköping, Sweden, has served as a freelance cartoonist since 1963. He specializes in political cartoons and caricatures. Ander has worked for a number of Swedish newspapers, including the *Norrköpings Tidningar*, *Östgöta Correspondenten* and *Svenska Dagbladet*. His cartoons have been syndicated through the Swedish News Agency to around seventy conservative and liberal papers.

Ander holds a postgraduate degree in graphic design from the Konstfack University College of Arts, Crafts, and Design. He is co-founder and former CEO and Chief Creative Officer of Kreab—today an international PR-company. He is also one of the founders and former president of the Swedish Verbovisual Academy.

Ander has illustrated a number of publications and published five books with political cartoons. He is also the author of *The Third Language—Communicating with All Senses*.

Ander lives in the countryside not far from Stockholm. His drawings are distributed on his own blog, by social media, and by News Agencies in Sweden, Europe, and the United States.

Matt Davies

Born in London, England, Davies moved to the United States in the mid-eighties. He studied illustration and fine art at both The Savannah College of Art & Design (Georgia) and The School of Visual Arts in New York City. Matt Davies is the editorial cartoonist for *Newsday* in New York. His work has been featured in many publications, including the *New York Times*, the *Washington Post*, the *Los Angeles Times*, and *USA Today*. His work has also appeared in *Newsweek*, *Time Magazine*, *U.S. News & World Report*, on CNN and in *Mad Magazine*. Matt is also a noted author and illustrator of children's books.

He is the recipient of many journalism awards for his work, notably the Pulitzer Prize (2004), the Herblock Prize (2004), the Robert F. Kennedy Journalism prize and the National Headliners Award (2017). He is a five-time recipient of the Society of Professional Journalists Deadline Club Award, including the 2001 prize for his work confronting a post 9/11 New York, and was honored with five first-place awards in the New York Associated Press Editorial Cartooning Competition. He was also a finalist for the Pulitzer Prize in both 2011 and 2016. His cartoons are syndicated internationally by Andrews McMeel Syndicate.

Joel Pett

Four-time Pulitzer finalist and 2000 Pulitzer prize-winner Joel Pett has been at the *Lexington Herald-Leader* since 1984. His sharp-edged political cartoons have appeared in hundreds of newspapers, including the *Washington Post*, the *New York Times*, the *Los Angeles Times*, the *Times of London*, *USA Today* and the *Katmandu Times*.

Other media credits include NPR's *All Things Considered*, *Morning Edition*, and *The World*; PBS' *Newshour*; MSNBC's *All In with Chris Hayes*, and magazines: *Time*, *Newsweek*, *Businessweek*, *Omni*, *Institutional Investor*, *Spa Finder*, *Sierra*, and *MAD*.

Pett also received the 1999 Robert F. Kennedy Journalism Award, and five Global Media Awards for cartoons on population issues, as well as an Emmy for television commentary. He is a past president of the Association of American Editorial Cartoonists, a past Pulitzer juror, and has conducted three overseas seminars on editorial cartooning as a guest speaker of the U.S. State Department.

A sometime stand-up comic, Pett has shared his blend of deceptively simple and provocative humor at dozens of venues, including the Newseum in Washington, D.C., Boston's John F. Kennedy Library, Indiana University, Whitman College, Ohio State University, Brandeis University, and more.

©Clay Bennett.
Chattanooga Times Free Press

Clay Bennett

Born January 20, 1958 in Clinton, South Carolina, the son of a career army officer, Bennett led a nomadic life, attending ten different schools before graduating in 1976 from S. R. Butler High School in Huntsville, Alabama.

Clay served as editorial cartoonist for his college paper and managing editor of the alternative student newspaper while attending the University of North Alabama, where he graduated in 1980 with degrees in art and history.

After working briefly as a staff artist for the *Pittsburgh Post-Gazette* and the (North Carolina) *Fayetteville Times,* Bennett went on to serve as the editorial cartoonist for the *St. Petersburg Times* (1981–1994) and the *Christian Science Monitor* (1997–2007). He now draws five cartoons a week for the *Chattanooga Times Free Press,* having joined its staff in 2008.

Recipient of The Pulitzer Prize for Editorial Cartooning in 2002, Bennett has earned almost every honor his profession has to offer, including the Sigma Delta Chi Award (2001), the National Journalism Award (2002), the Robert F. Kennedy Award (2007), the United Nations/Ranan Lurie Award (2011), the Grambs Aronson Award (2013), the Berryman Award (2014) the John Fischetti Award (2001, 2005), the Overseas Press Club Award (2005, 2007), and the National Headliner Award (1999, 2000, 2004, 2016).

Past president of the Association of American Editorial Cartoonists, Bennett is the husband of artist Cindy Procious and the father of Matt, Ben, and Sarah. His work is distributed internationally by the Washington Post Writers Group.

'Haven't we suffered enough?'

Walt Handelsman

Walt Handelsman is the two-time Pulitzer Prize-winning editorial cartoonist for the *Advocate*. His work is nationally syndicated by the Tribune Content Agency in Chicago to over 200 newspapers around the country and internationally. One of the most widely reprinted cartoonists in America, Handelsman's work has been seen in *Newsweek*, *Time*, and the *Chicago Tribune*. He has been a featured guest on CNN, *The Newshour* and ABC's *Nightline*.

Mr. Handelsman has won every major journalism award for cartooning excellence, including the 1989 and 1993 National Headliner award, the 1992 and 2014 Society of Professional Journalists Award, The 1996 Robert F. Kennedy Journalism Award, The 2003 Scripps Howard National Journalism Award, The 2007 Online Journalism Award, and in 1997 and 2007, the Pulitzer Prize.

In 2006, Walt taught himself flash animation and in 2007 became the first person to win the Pulitzer Prize for animation. Before joining the *Advocate* in 2013, Walt worked for *Newsday* in New York (2001–2013), the *New Orleans Times-Picayune* (1989–2001) the *Scranton Times* (1985–1989) and a chain of thirteen Baltimore and Washington weekly papers. (1982–1985). He holds a general studies degree in advertising from the University of Cincinnati.

Walt is author of seven collections of his editorial cartoons, as well as a children's book published in 1995. He and his family live in New Orleans.

Jack Ohman

Jack Hamilton Ohman was born on September 1, 1960 in St. Paul, Minnesota. He is the editorial cartoonist and Associate Editor for the *Sacramento Bee*. His work appears in 200 newspapers through the Tribune Content Agency. Ohman was, at age nineteen, the youngest editorial cartoonist ever nationally syndicated. He has worked at the *Columbus Dispatch*, the *Detroit Free Press*, and the *Oregonian*.

Ohman won the 2016 Pulitzer Prize, and was a Pulitzer finalist in 2012. He has won virtually every major award in American journalism. Besides the Pulitzer Prize, Ohman has won the Robert F. Kennedy Journalism Award, the Society of Professional Journalists Sigma Delta Chi Award, the SDX Mark of Excellence Award, the National Headliner Award, the Overseas Press Club Award, the Scripps Howard Foundation Award, and two first place Best of the West Awards. He also won The Minnesota Daily Harrison E. Salisbury Distinguished Alumni Award.

Ohman has a B.A. in History from the University Honors Program at Portland State University. He is the author of eleven books, four on the subject of fly fishing. He writes editorials and regular columns as well.

He is married and has three children.

Mark Fiore

Pulitzer Prize-winner, Mark Fiore, who the *Wall Street Journal* has called "the undisputed guru of the form," creates cartoons in San Francisco, one of the most fertile regions for creating observational and satirical cartoons. His work has appeared on the *San Francisco Chronicle's* website, Newsweek.com, Slate.com, CBSNews.com, MotherJones.com, NPR's web site, and is currently featured by KQED. Fiore's political animation has appeared on CNN, PBS, *Bill Moyers Journal*, Salon.com and cable and broadcast outlets across the globe.

Fiore's work has appeared in publications ranging from the *Washington Post* to the *Los Angeles Times*. In the late 1990s, he began to experiment with animating political cartoons, and, after a short stint at the *San Jose Mercury News* as their staff cartoonist, Fiore devoted much of his energy to animation. Mark majored in political science at Colorado College, where, in a perfect send off for a cartoonist, he received his diploma in 1991 as commencement speaker Dick Cheney smiled approvingly.

Mark Fiore was awarded the Pulitzer Prize for political cartooning in 2010, a Robert F. Kennedy Journalism Award in 2004 and has twice received an Online Journalism Award for commentary from the Online News Association (2002, 2008). Fiore has received two awards for his work in new media from the National Cartoonists Society (2001, 2002), and in 2006 received The James Madison Freedom of Information Award from The Society of Professional Journalists.

Mike Keefe

Mike Keefe, born November 6, 1946 in Santa Rosa, California, was the editorial cartoonist for the *Denver Post*, 1975–2011. Since 2012 he has been a regular contributor to the *Colorado Independent*, an online news site. His cartoons are syndicated by Cagle Cartoons and have appeared in *Time, Newsweek, Businessweek, U.S. News & World Report*, the *New York Times*, the *Washington Post*, and hundreds of newspapers across the country.

He won the Pulitzer Prize for Editorial Cartooning in 2011. Other honors include: The National Headliner's Award, Sigma Delta Chi Distinguished Service Award, The Best of the West Journalism Contest, The National Press Association Berryman Award, and the Fischetti Cartoon Competition. Keefe served as president of the Association of American Editorial cartoonists and is a former John S. Knight Fellow at Stanford University.

Before becoming a cartoonist, Keefe spent one year on an auto assembly line and two years in the United States Marine Corps. He earned B.S. and M.S. degrees and completed course work for a Ph.D. in Mathematics at the University of Missouri, Kansas City. Keefe has played guitar and harmonica in a number of rock and blues bands for decades. He and his wife, Anita Austin, have two grown children and live in San Miguel de Allende, Mexico.

Luo Jie

Luo Jie, known by the pen name of Luojie, is an award-winning cartoonist from one of the world's most fascinating and complex countries, China. He lives in Beijing, China and has been working at the *China Daily* since 2002. He is deputy chief of the art department at the *China Daily* and draws cartoons for the comments page. The *China Daily* has a readership in the billions. He has the distinction of winning the Chinese News Award for cartoons eight times. His motto is: "Only in political cartoons, I am alive."

In an interview with chinadaily.com on August 29, 2013, Luojie said, "I like painting, especially foreign political cartoons, since I was young. I dream of drawing some exaggerated but excellent cartoons. Before I knew 'Painter,' I just drew for fun and had no regular time to practice my drawing skills. Later, I learned how to draw cartoons by computer with 'Painter,' and I was surprised to find that I was talented in drawing. I made great progress in the field and joined professional circles. I am good at making up for the shortages that come from my basic skills. My experience in computer drawing is that you need to correct until you feel satisfied. Speaking of innovation, I think we should learn more from others—learn to compare and practice."

Luojie's cartoons are internationally syndicated by Cagle Cartoons.

Michel Kichka

Michel Kichka, born August 15, 1954 in Seraing, Belgium, emigrated to Israel in 1974. He graduated from the Bezalel Academy of Arts & Design in the visual communication department in 1978. He has been a professor and has taught illustration, comics, and cartoon art there since 1983. He is an Israeli editorial cartoonist best known for his work of the last twenty years for several television channels such as Israel Channel 1 and 2, TV5 Monde, i24NEWS, France 24, as well as for magazines such as *Courrier International* (France) and *Regards* (Belgium).

Kichka is a member of Cartooning for Peace Association. He was the chairman of the Israeli Cartoonists Association in the years 2004–2010. He took part in the creation of the Comics and Cartoon Museum of Holon near Tel Aviv in 2006. Kichka won the Dosh Award for best Israeli cartoonist in 2008, the International Toons Mag Award (Norway) in 2016 and the Saint-Just Award (France) in 2016. Kichka is also a graphic novel author. His book, *Second Generation—The Things I Did Not Tell My Father*, has been published in nine languages. The book is being made into an animated film in France, directed by Vera Belmont.

He lives in Jerusalem with his wife Olivia. They have three sons and three grandchildren.

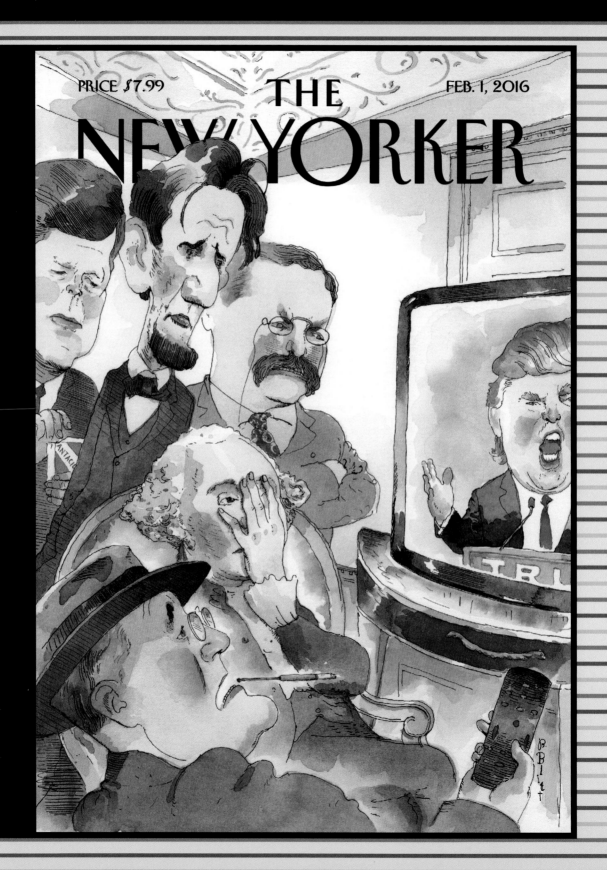

PRICE $7.99

FEB. 1, 2016

THE NEW YORKER

Barry Blitt

Barry Blitt, born April 30, 1958 in Montreal, Canada, is a cartoonist and an illustrator. Since 1992, he has contributed illustrations and more than one hundred covers to the *New Yorker*, including "Deluged," which was voted Cover of the Year by the American Society of Magazine Editors in 2006, and "The Politics of Fear," a finalist for the same award in 2009. His work has also appeared in *Vanity Fair*, *Time*, *Rolling Stone*, and the *Atlantic*. Blitt illustrated Frank Rich's weekly column in the *New York Times*.

He has been honored with exhibitions and awards from the Society of Illustrators, *Print*, and *American Illustration*, and is a member of the Art Directors Club Hall of Fame.

Blitt's work for children includes, *You Never Heard of Casey Stengel?!*, *George Washington's Birthday*, *While You Were Napping*, *Baby's First Tattoo: A Memory Book for Modern Parents*, and *Once Upon a Time, the End (Asleep in 60 Seconds)*.

Later this year, Riverhead Books will publish *Blitt*, a retrospective collection of his illustration career.